☀ INSIGHT COMPACT GUIDE

ITALIAN LAKES

Compact Guide: Italian Lakes is the ultimate quick-reference guide to this alluring destination. It tells you all you need to know about the region's attractions, from medieval towns and their castles to magnificent Renaissance villas and their gardens, from the relaxation of the lakeshore to hikes through the mountains.

This is one of 130 Compact Guides from one of the world's best known information providers: Insight Guides, whose titles have set the standard for visual travel guides since 1970.

D1146783

APA PUBLICATIONS L

Part of the Langenscheidt Publishing Group

Insight Compact Guide: Italian Lakes

Written by: Christine Hamel, Eva Gründel and Heinz Tomek
English version by: David Ingram
Updated by: Adele Evans
Edited by: Rachel Fox
Photography by: George Taylor and Annabel Elston
Cover picture by: Fototeca, 9x12
Picture Editor: Hilary Genin
Maps: Polyglott

Editorial Director: Brian Bell
Managing Editor: Tony Halliday

CONTACTING THE EDITORS: As every effort is made to provide accurate information in this publication, we would appreciate it if readers would call our attention to any errors and omissions by contacting:
Apa Publications, PO Box 7910, London SE1 1WE, England.
Fax: (44 20) 7403 0290
e-mail: insight@apaguide.co.uk

Information has been obtained from sources believed to be reliable, but its accuracy and completeness, and the opinions based thereon, are not guaranteed.

© 2008 APA Publications GmbH & Co. Verlag KG Singapore Branch, Singapore.

Second Edition 2002; Updated 2008
Printed in Singapore by Insight Print Services (Pte) Ltd
Original edition © Polyglott-Verlag Dr Bolte KG, Munich

Worldwide distribution enquiries:
APA Publications GmbH & Co. Verlag KG (Singapore Branch)
38 Joo Koon Road, Singapore 628990
Tel: (65) 6865 1600, Fax: (65) 6861 6438

Distributed in the UK & Ireland by:
GeoCenter International Ltd
Meridian House, Churchill Way West, Basingstoke,
Hampshire RG21 6YR
Tel: (44) 1256 817987, Fax: (44) 1256 817988

Distributed in the United States by:
Langenscheidt Publishers, Inc.
36–36 33rd Street 4th Floor
Long Island City, NY 11106
Tel: (1) 718 784 0055, Fax: (1) 718 784 0640

www.insightguides.com

Introduction

Places

Culture

Travel Tips

△ **Colleoni Chapel (p66)**
World-famous carvings from
Bergamo's loveliest church.

▽ **San Zeno Maggiore
(p102)** Verona's magnificent Romanesque basilica.

△ **Locarno (p20)**
This attractive Swiss city has
a wonderfully mild climate
and a great location.

▷ **Borromean Islands
(p27)** Famous islands
in Lake Maggiore, with
beautiful villas and gardens.

◁ **Bellagio (p59)**
With its dramatic location
at the point where Lake
Como and Lake Lecco
divide, Bellagio is a stunning
town, loved by writers and
artists, and famous for its
villas and parks.

△ **Santa Caterina del Sasso (p31)** A 12th-century chapel and pilgrimage site with a dramatic location on Lake Maggiore.

▽ **Sirmione (p83)** A fairytale town on Lake Garda, home to the impressive moated Scaligeri Castle.

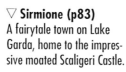

△ **Malcescine (p76)** Attractive harbour town on Lake Garda, complete with castle and palace.

▽ **Villa Carlotta (p56)** A lavishly decorated villa with beautiful gardens.

◁ **Lugano (p38)** This beautifully situated town on the lake of the same name is famous for its mild climate and is full of cultural attractions.

A Region for all Tastes

The Northern Italian Lakes are one of the most fascinating regions of Italy, and also one of the most popular with tourists. Their waters ensure that winters stay pleasantly mild, and summers pleasantly cool. Their shores are lined with elegant villas surrounded by delightful parks and gardens. The region is also justly famed for its magnificent views and vistas, and a drive through this part of Italy is often a challenge to intrepid motorists as well as being an unforgettable visual treat.

The Northern Italian Lakes – Maggiore, Como, Lugano, Garda and the many smaller ones, in total 297 – are surrounded by the Swiss Ticino and the Italian regions of Lombardy and Piedmont, all of them areas steeped in history and with no end of superb cultural sights to visit, ranging from prehistoric remains and Roman ruins to finely crafted Lombard Romanesque churches and magnificent Renaissance architecture.

The lakes region, where Italy meets the Alps and northern Europe, has always been of enormous strategic importance historically, and the beautiful landscape is enhanced still further by dozens of castles and fortresses, including those built by Verona's most famous medieval family, the Scaligeri, along the shores of Lake Garda. Verona has almost as many ancient sites as Rome itself, while Bergamo owes its architectural beauty and harmony to the many years of Venetian rule there. These cities, and also many of the smaller towns, contain first-class art galleries, with priceless paintings by artists such as Titian, Raphael, Tintoretto and Mantegna.

A Place for Connoisseurs

In the days before mass tourism, Lake Como in particular was a holiday retreat for British connoisseurs of good taste, including a smattering of famous writers. Wordsworth lived there in 1790, Byron and Shelley were both regular visitors, and D.H. Lawrence made it his home from 1925 to

Opposite: Isola di Garda
Below: Lavertezzo bathers
Bottom: Santa Caterina del Sasso detail

Below: views wherever you look
Bottom: sunbathing near Morcote, Lake Lugano

1927. Visitors today can not only bask in the extraordinary cultural landscape and scenery that the region possesses, but also enjoy many modern outdoor activities, such as windsurfing, water-skiing and golf.

Hikers and climbers can take to the mountains, while those in search of relaxation can sunbathe on the shore or enjoy the spectacular views from the deck of a steamer. In addition to all this, the region is justly famed for its food and its wines, many of which bear familiar names such as Bardolino, Valpolicella and Soave.

These are just a few of the reasons why the Italian Lakes have exerted such an irresistible attraction on tourists for so many years now. And last but not least of course, there are the Italians themselves, who have maintained their way of life despite the tourist onslaught. Welcome to one of the most beautiful and exciting parts of Italy.

POSITION AND LANDSCAPE

The lakes lie in Upper Italy between the Lombardy Plain and the high Alps. Each lake has its own individual character and shape: they are all long and thin (known as ribbon lakes), but Maggiore, the second largest lake (66km/41 miles long), has a kink in it like the hind leg of a horse, Lugano and Como resemble upside down 'Y's, while Garda, the largest lake in Italy (51km/33 miles long), has a bulbous bottom. All these shapes are the result of complex local geology and the process of glaciation that took place during the Ice Age *(see opposite)*. While the southern end of Lake Garda extends into the plain, Lake Como is surrounded by mountains. Even though it is only the third-largest lake in Upper Italy (50km/32 miles long), Como is the deepest lake in Europe (410m/1,350ft).

Though not as high as the central Alps, the mountains surrounding the lakes provide an impressive backdrop. The summit of Monte Legnone (2,609m/8,560ft) towers more than

2,400m (7,900ft) over the surface of Lake Como – at a horizontal distance of only 6km (4 miles) from the shore. It is the highest summit in the area, but there are other impressive and beautiful massifs around Como, notably the limestone Grigna (2,409m/7,903ft). The Ticino Alps around Lake Maggiore to the west, though not quite so high, still have some fine peaks, including the Gridone (2,188m/7,178ft) and Monte Zeda (2,156m/7,070ft). Away to the east, Lake Garda is separated from the Adige valley by the narrow ridge of Monte Baldo which rises almost 2,000m (6,500ft) above the lake.

Lake Maggiore is drained by the Ticino river, Lake Como by the Adda, Lake Garda by the Mincio. All of them are tributaries of the Po, which flows into the Adriatic.

GEOLOGICAL HISTORY

Some 350 million years ago, much of present-day Upper Italy was covered by a tropical sea. As the marine life died it was deposited on the sea bed, where it consolidated in layers, until around 60 million years ago when massive movements of the earth's crust resulted in the creation of the Alps. Around 2 million years ago, during the Pleistocene period, the rivers that flowed into the Po from the Apennines and the

Below: Val Cannobina above Lake Maggiore
Bottom: Como's Villa dell' Olmo and Tempio Voltano

Alps brought a great deal of alluvial silt with them; this was deposited on the Plain of Lombardy and is the reason why the whole area has remained so fertile to this day.

THE ICE AGE

Views of Lake Garda

Before the last Ice Age, *circa* 9000BC, there were no lakes in the region, but simply large valleys. During this Ice Age, the rivers became powerful glaciers, and massive basins were gouged out of the rock. The level of the bottom of these new basins was considerably lower than that of the exit to the valleys, so after the glaciers retreated and the valleys filled up with water, the resulting lakes were extremely deep, their bottoms lying well below sea level.

Additional depth was created by the morraine debris the glaciers left behind as they retreated. The deepest part of Lake Garda, for instance, is 346m (1,135ft), with the moraine thickness of 149m (488ft) making up almost half of that. The glaciers left behind not only lakes but also highly complex drainage patterns seen, for example, in the two arms of Lake Como, one of which has no outflow at all, and in Lake Orta to the west of Lake Maggiore, which drains out to the north.

The mountains defining the lakes are not of uniform structure. To the north of Lake Garda, they are formed of a specialised form of limestone

known as dolomite. Between Garda and Como, the prevalent rock is granite, whose resistance to erosion explains the fact that no large lake has been formed in that area. Around Como and Maggiore, it's largely limestone again, though intrusions of crystalline rock (schists and gneiss) become more pronounced the further west you go.

CLIMATE

The Mediterranean-type climate of the Italian lakes is one of the main reasons tourists are so attracted to the area. Despite their central European location and proximity to the Alps, the lakes are so large that they create a micro-climate, making winters warmer than is usual for this latitude and summers slightly cooler. However, because of the mountain environment, the weather on Lakes Maggiore, Como and particularly Garda isn't all that predictable: in spring and autumn, be prepared for sudden cloudbursts (which are most likely to occur in May and September).

Even in January, snowfalls are very rare at lake level and temperatures average 3–7°C (37–45°F). By the beginning of April the sun is as warm as it is elsewhere in Europe in mid-May. In the summer a fresh breeze keeps the temperatures pleasant even when there isn't a cloud in the sky. The relatively steady winds blowing up and down the lakes make them a paradise for windsurfers and sailors.

WHEN TO GO

Many like to visit the lakes in the springtime, when there is a profusion of blossom, and the villas with their parks and gardens are utterly magnificent. Swimmers tend to favour early summer through to September as a good time for a holiday.

The water is a very pleasant 25°C (77°F) during July and August. Autumn is ideal for long hikes and serene contemplation of (relatively) tourist-free scenery, and the service is a lot better in the restaurants because the staff have more time. Winter is quiet, and many places close down for the season.

Gardens
The region's mild climate and plentiful water make it ideal for gardeners. Proof of this lies in the many beautiful gardens found around the shores of the lakes – often the grounds of sumptuous villas.

Villa Carlotta Gardens in Tremezzo

CLIMATE CHART

Verbania (Pallanza)

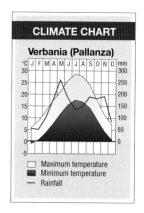

☐ Maximum temperature
■ Minimum temperature
— Rainfall

Language

Un omm al gheva a düü fiö ('A man had two sons') could be the opening of any local fairytale, and anyone who's just done a course in Italian will be annoyed to discover that he or she doesn't understand a word. The strange language is Lombardian. Never fear, however: only a few small communities high in the mountains continue to communicate in it exclusively. The language of Dante – which marked the beginning of Italian literature – was Tuscan, and over the centuries Lombardian was gradually squeezed out by Tuscan Italian as the favoured dialect. However, generally regional dialect will be used first.

FLORA AND FAUNA

In January, when everything north of the Alps is usually under a blanket of snow, jasmine and laurel are already blooming in Northern Italy. In February, the mimosa and forsythia herald the spring with their intense yellow blossom, and in March the camellias, magnolias, oleander, gorse and peach-trees all burst into blossom. The whole scene is reminiscent of the Mediterranean, and it's hard to believe that such splendour actually exists miles inland.

The vegetation is as varied as the local fauna. Reptiles are common, especially lizards and the odd snake. A lot of animals are active at night, such as wild boar, foxes and bats.

All of the lakes continue to have an abundance of fish despite the pressures of industry, tourism and fishing. Species include trout, eel, carp, perch and whitefish. However, until urgent remedial action was taken recently by the authorities, fish stocks were under serious threat from water pollution.

AGRICULTURE AND INDUSTRY

Summer grazing

Lombardy is considered the 'powerhouse of Italy', and so it's no wonder that the towns along the edge of the Alps (Varese, Como, Lecco) are largely industrial. The most obviously industrial areas are in the Brianza and around Como; the latter, chiefly famous as the *città della seta* (city of silk), has diversified a lot over the past few decades and become as industrial as Varese. Iron-working has taken over from silk as the main industry around Lake Como.

As far as agriculture is concerned, the higher plains are suited to the cultivation of cereals, including maize (for polenta), green vegetables and fruit trees. The hilly zone has fruit and chestnut trees, and the soil around the lakes is especially suitable for olive trees and citrus fruits. Vines grow at an altitude of up to 850m (2,400ft), and on the Alpine meadows there is excellent grazing for both cattle (half of which are milk producing) and sheep (bred for wool as well as meat).

TOURISM

A vital part of the economy is tourism. Lake Garda alone has more than 5 million foreign visitors a year. The sheer wealth of cultural sights, combined with the astonishing variety of activities on offer, acts as an irresistible magnet to tourists from all over the world; one reason why summer accommodation beside any of the lakes should be booked well in advance.

However, not all the inhabitants of the region have gained from its prosperity. Whenever you travel a short distance inland from the roads around these lakes it becomes clear just how depopulated many of the villages in the rural areas have become.

The steep peaks and deep ravines, so picturesque for the traveller, are often part of a never-ending struggle for survival for the poor people living in regions like the Grigna. Young people have been leaving for generations now, heading for the towns and big cities to set up a new life for themselves in safer and more comfortable surroundings. Only recently has there been a movement among young people *away* from the smog and hectic lifestyle found in the urban centres, and back to the peace of the countryside – and it is growing steadily more popular. With revenue from tourism, the prospect of making a living away from the cities has become viable.

Below: rural life
Bottom: streets around the castle in Malcesine

HISTORICAL HIGHLIGHTS

9000BC Settlers arrive in the Po Valley.

7th century BC Celt settlements established that later develop into cities, including Milan, Como and Bergamo. The Celts trade with the Etruscans.

4th century BC The Gauls cross the Alps, sacking Rome in 390BC.

3rd century BC The Romans drive out the Gauls to take control of northern Italy.

191BC The region becomes the Roman province of Gallia Cisalpina. The capital is Mediolanum (Milan). The Romans lay the foundations of the industrial triangle between Milan, Genoa and Turin.

2nd century BC Bergamo and Como both become Roman colonies.

89BC Verona becomes a Roman colony.

59–49BC Under the governorship of Caesar, Verona becomes strategically and commercially important.

AD286 Diocletian assigns Milan as residence and main administrative centre to his emperor-colleague, Maximian.

AD313 Under the Edict of Milan, Constantine the Great grants freedom of worship to Christians.

4th century AD Upper Italian lakes become a transit region for French and English pilgrims on their way to Rome.

AD330 Constantine moves the capital of the Empire to Byzantium.

5th century Following the division of the Empire into two halves in 393, the west becomes vulnerable to attacks by tribes from central Europe.

403 Verona is besieged by the Visigoths.

452 The forces of Attila the Hun lay waste to Verona and the Po Valley.

476 End of the western Empire. The Germanic leader Odoacer conquers northern Italy.

568 The Lombards invade northern Italy and take control of all the cities north of the River Po and the lake.

774 Charlemagne is summoned by the pope. He destroys the Lombard kingdom and creates a Frankish state in north Italy.

9th–10th centuries Bishops of some cities obtain sovereign privileges, exercising civil and ecclesiastical rule.

962 Otto I retakes Italy, the start of almost 200 years of German domination.

11th–16th centuries The Italian city states. Milan, Bergamo and Verona thrive from trade with Asia. Power moves from the merchants to a few local families *(Signori)*.

11th–12th centuries Milan battles against its less prosperous neighbours.

1118–27 In the Ten Years' War, Milan virtually destroys Como.

1164 The Veronese League is formed to prevent Barbarossa gaining control of Lombardy. It becomes the basis of the Lombard League, established in 1167.

1176 Barbarossa is defeated by the Lombard League at Legnano. By the Peace of Constance in 1183, he is forced to accept the independence of the city states.

1262 The rise of the Scaligeri family; Mastino becomes mayor of Verona.

1277 Mastino I della Scala is murdered, but the Venetians immediately replace him with his tyrannical brother, Alberto.

1278–1447 The Visconti rule Milan.

1311–29 Cangrande I della Scala extends his sphere of influence.

1335 The Visconti take over Como.

1352 The hated Cangrande II della Scala assumes power, and is murdered seven years later by his brother Cansignorio.

1387 Scaligeri rule comes to an end when Verona is besieged by the Visconti.

1405–1521 Venice conquers Brescia, Verona and Lake Garda.

1450 Francesco Sforza, son-in-law of the last Visconti, assumes power in Milan and Como.

1496–1500 The area of modern-day Ticino is annexed by Switzerland.

1500–25 Milan is claimed by France, Germany and Venice. Emperor Charles V installs another Sforza as duke.

1535 After the death of the last Sforza duke, Milan falls to Spain.

1796 Napoleon takes Lombardy and the Veneto. In 1797 the Cisalpine Republic is formed by the Treaty of Campoformio.

1814–15 Napoleon is defeated. At the Congress of Vienna, Lombardy and the Veneto are ceded to Austria.

Early 19th century Italians under Austrian rule and 'free' Italians of Piedmont begin to campaign for an independent Italy. In 1842, a newspaper, *Il Risorgimento (The Awakening)*, gives its name to Garibaldi's independence movement.

1848–66 The Risorgimento fights against Austrian rule.

1859 They win a decisive victory at the Battle of Solferino, south of Lake Garda.

1861 Vienna surrenders Lombardy and the Veneto to the new Kingdom of Italy.

1919 The Treaty of Saint-Germain gives the northern shore of Lake Garda, the Trentino and southern Tyrol to Italy, which extends to the Brenner Pass. Mussolini establishes fascist brigades in Milan and gains power three years later.

1943–45 The collapse of the northern front. Mussolini retires to Lake Garda and founds the 'Republic of Salò'. On 28 April 1945 he is caught fleeing to Switzerland, and executed.

1946 Italy becomes a republic; the discredited Savoy royal family is exiled.

1993 Lake Maggiore floods.

1996 A centre-left coalition *(Ulivo)* wins local and regional elections.

2000 Floods in Lake Maggiore area.

2001 Silvio Berlusconi, right-wing media mogul, is elected prime minister.

2002 Italy adopts the euro.

2003 Members of the Savoy family are allowed to return to Italy. Financial scandal erupts as the huge food company Parmalat is declared bankrupt.

2005 Pope John Paul II dies and is succeeded by Benedictus XVI.

2006 Romano Prodi narrowly defeats Silvio Berlusconi as prime minister. His centre-left coalition has a majority of just two seats in the Senate.

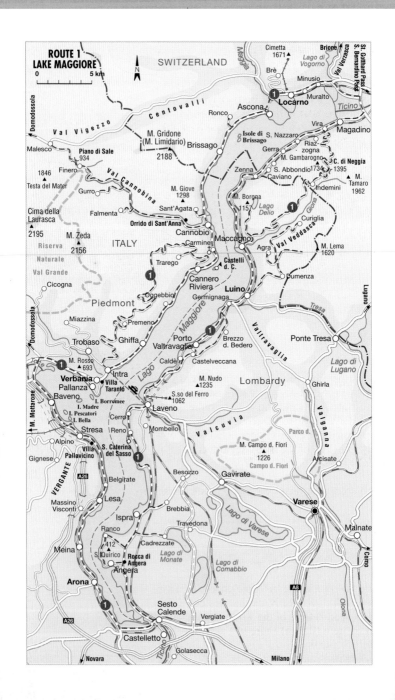

1: Lake Maggiore

Map on page 18

Lake Maggiore was known as *Lacus Verbanus* in Ancient Rome, and fragrant verbena still grows on its shores. It is much praised as a natural wonder and a popular holiday destination, and for many vistors epitomises the region. Like all the lakes south of the Alps, Lake Maggiore owes its existence to Ice Age glaciers which hollowed out its base to a depth of 372m (1,220ft) – or a full 179m (587ft) below sea-level.

With a surface area of 216sq m (2,324sq ft), Lake Maggiore is the second-largest of the Northern Italian Lakes after Lake Garda; it is 66km (41 miles) long, with an average width of between 4km (2 miles) and 11km (6 miles). The lake's most important river is the Ticino, which has its source in the Alps of Central Switzerland and flows into Lake Maggiore near Locarno. The Ticino river also drains the lake, flowing into the Po not far from Pavia.

The Garden of Europe
Lake Maggiore isn't just sunshine, water and mountains. Since the 17th century, when it became a favoured destination of the privileged few, it has been one of the most important routes between the Alpine passes and the Po valley. Today the magnificent villas and parks by Lake Maggiore, nicknamed the 'garden of Europe', draw visitors from all sections of society.

Preceding pages: Lake Orta
Below: taking the high road
Bottom: smile from Val Cannobina

BACKGROUND

Lake Maggiore is shared by Italy and Switzerland: the upper fifth of it is Swiss and forms part of the canton of Ticino; the western shore is part of the Italian region of Piedmont (province of Novara); and the eastern shore belongs to Lombardy (province of Varese). The northern part of the lake is surrounded by high mountains, such as the Gridone (2,188m/7,178ft), but opens up towards the south, unveiling its special attractions as it does so. The mountains form a dramatic backdrop, and the southern sun bathes the landscape in brilliant light.

With its towns of Locarno, Ascona, Verbania and Stresa, the Piedmont shore is more wealthy than the less developed eastern shore. The latter, on the other hand, has more unspoilt natural scenery. The prosperity of the western shore attracts about a third of the working population of the eastern (Italian) shore of Lake Maggiore work in Switzerland, who commute between the two countries daily.

Map
on page
18

Below: lakeshore at Locarno
Bottom: Locarno view

The Western Shore

Locarno – Ascona – Brissago – Cannobio (57km/35 miles)

★★**Locarno** (pop. 14,000), the capital of the Swiss canton, vies with Lugano for the title of finest town in the Ticino. The magnificent landscape at the upper end of Lake Maggiore and the mild, fog-free climate has attracted northern European tourists since the 19th century. The town prospered after World War II, and now includes the suburbs of Muralto, Minusio, Orselina and Brione.

Today the shore of Lake Maggiore is built up from the Maggia to the Verzasca, but Locarno still retains much of its charm – a special combination of Swiss-Alpine and Southern-Italian.

HISTORY

The region round Locarno was probably inhabited in prehistoric times, but was certainly settled during the Roman era. The first written mention of the town dates from AD789. Over the centuries, Locarno profited from its strategic location at the northern end of Lake Maggiore, on the trading route leading across the great Alpine passes. It received its charter from the emperor Barbarossa in 1189, and passed into the hands of the Viscontis of Milan in 1342. In 1513 it was conquered

by the Swiss Confederation, and after the fall of
the Ancien Regime (1798) it became a part of
the Swiss canton of Lugano. From 1803 to 1878
it then shared the status as Ticino's capital alter-
nately with Lugano and Bellinzona.

Star Attraction
• Locarno

PIAZZA GRANDE

At the centre of Locarno is the **Piazza Grande**,
where the traditional market is held every second
Tuesday; the square dates from the 19th century.
The 14th-century Torre del Comune forms part
of the line of houses on the side facing the mountains; to the east is the municipal park with the
theatre. Down the Via Franchino Rusca is the
★ **Castello Visconteo**, still one of the most important castles in the Ticino despite being largely
destroyed by the Confederation in 1532.

It was founded in medieval times, and today
houses the **Museo Civico** (open Apr–Oct Tues–
Sun 10am–6pm), with its extensive collections of
local archaeological finds and Romanesque sculpture. The historic town centre is a great place for
a stroll: one of the finest townhouses is the **Casa
Rusca** in Piazza S. Antonio, containing the Pina-
coteca Comunale (open Apr–mid-Dec Tues–Sun
10am–5pm), which has an important Dada collection by Hans Arp.

One of Locarno's more recent attractions is the
★ **Falconeria Locarno** on Via delle Scuole (open
mid-Mar–mid-Nov Tues–Sun 9.30–noon and 1.30–
4.30pm; falconry shows at 10.15am and 3pm, June–
end Aug at 10.15am, 4pm & 6pm; www.falconeria.ch).

In August Locarno hosts the popular and influential International Film Festival.

> **Locarno churches**
> Of the churches in the old
> town, **Santa Maria in
> Selva** is well known for its Late
> Gothic ★ choir frescoes, showing
> Scenes from the Life of Christ, but the
> most famous sacred structure on the
> northern shore of Lake Maggiore is
> without doubt the church of ★★ **San
> Vittore** in Muralto, not far from the
> railway station. This three-aisled
> Romanesque pillared basilica dates
> from between 1090 and 1110, and
> the Romanesque ★★ crypt with its
> fascinating capitals is definitely worth
> a visit.

Monk at Madonna del Sasso

MADONNA DEL SASSO

Above Locarno stands the famous 15th-century
pilgrimage church of **Madonna del Sasso** (open
daily 7am–6pm). At 365m (1,200ft), the site dou-
bles as a superb observation point for the city,
mountains and lake. It can be reached by road or
by funicular (tram), or, for the more energetic,
by the old Way of the Cross. The present pilgrim-

Map on page 18

Famous vegetarians
The **Percorso Museale del Monte Verità** in Ascona (open Apr–Oct Tues–Sun 3–6pm), headquarters of the 'Vegetarian Cooperative of Ascona' from 1900 to 1920, contains much information on all the reformists and thinkers, including the psychologist C.G. Jung and the flamboyant dancer Isadora Duncan, who came here to 'get away from it all' in the early 20th century.

Hidden Ascona

age church of Santa Maria Assunta dates from the 16th and 17th centuries, and the main attraction of the interior is Bramantino's *Flight from Egypt* (1520). A cable car takes you from the church of Madonna del Sasso to the Cardada plateau. But for the most spectacular view of the lake and snow-capped Alps continue on the chairlift to the summit of the plateau at 1,670m (5,480ft).

ASCONA

The mighty delta of the Maggia separates Locarno from the no less beautiful town of ★ **Ascona** (pop. 5,000). Still only a small fishing village before the turn of the 20th century, Ascona first became a paradise for theosophical 'seekers after truth', before becoming the cosmopolitan resort it is today. Picturesquely situated in a bay, the town has an unmistakeable flair of its own.

The parish church of **SS Pietro e Paolo** (open daily 9am–noon and 4–6.30pm), a 16th-century three-aisled pillared basilica, contains three magnificent ★ altar paintings by the local painter Giovanni Serodine (1594–1630), a pupil of Caravaggio, who lived next door in Ascona's finest baroque building, the ★ **Casa Borrani** (1620).

At the edge of the old town centre stands the **Collegio Paio**, founded in 1584, with a fine Renaissance courtyard and a magnificent ★ cloister. The church of **Santa Maria della Misericordia** contains several valuable ★ frescoes dating from the 15th and 16th centuries. High above Ascona is **Monte Verità** (320m/1,050ft), with a view across the lake and the Maggia delta.

BRISSAGO

The nearby town of **Brissago** has a very southern atmosphere, with all its palazzi and Mediterranean vegetation. Archaeological finds in the vicinity point to early settlement by the Celts, who were followed by the Romans. During the Middle Ages, Brissago was a miniature republic and enjoyed several privileges, such as tax exemption and its own legal system – rights which had to be fiercely defended during the 16th and 17th centuries, after it had joined the Confederation.

Today, tourism is Brissago's main source of income, and the historic centre is consequently losing much of its former charm. Sights worth seeing include the **Casa Branca** (1680–1720) with its magnificent facade; the church of ★ **Madonna del Ponte** (1520–45) just to the south of the town, a fine example of Lombardian architecture; and the famous **cigar factory** (Fabbrica Tabacchi) founded in 1847, also south of the town (guided tours May–Sept).

Below: Madonna del Ponte in Brissago
Bottom: ferry to Isola Grande

THE ISLANDS

The region around Brissago is ideal for hiking, with some fine views of the lake and the mighty massif of the Gridone in the distance. Don't miss the ★ **Brissago Islands**, either. They were probably inhabited as far back as Roman times, and a ruined church on the Isolino (the smaller island) dates from the 12th century.

The Isola Grande, properly known as 'Isola di San Pancrazio', has a magnificent ★ **botanical garden** (open Apr–Oct daily 9am–5pm), containing over 1,600 species, including some unique tropical and subtropical vegetation. The villa, built in an Italian Renaissance style in 1927, is now home to an art museum (open daily 9.30am–5pm).

Maps on pages 18 & 26

Below: the bustle of market day in Cannobio
Bottom: the peace of Val Cannobina

CANNOBIO

Across the border in Italy, **Cannobio** is a delightful place, with a historic centre, picturesque arcades next to the lake, and the pilgrimage church of **Santuario della Pietà** adjacent to the quayside. Designed by Pellegrino Tibaldi in 1571, it contains a supposedly miracle-working image of the *Mourning of Christ*. The 13th-century **Palazzo della Ragione**, the old town hall (closed to the public), houses a small exhibition centre under its portico.

Two km (1½ miles) from the town centre, the Cannnobino stream crashes through the wild ★ **Orrido di Sant'Anna** gorge. Between the Gridone and Monte Zeda, the ★★ **Val Cannobina** itself is well worth a detour, with tiny settlements and the odd church clinging to the mountain sides.

Continuing down the western shore, just before the popular resort of Cannero Riviera, two rocky islands, the **Castelli di Cannero**, jut out of the water. They were once the stronghold of the Mazzarditi brothers, who took over the existing castles on the islands in the early 15th century and terrorised lake travellers and lakeside dwellers with their piracy. The castles were razed to the ground in 1414 by Filippo Visconti; only the ruins remain.

From **Cannero Riviera** it is possible to take the mountain road to Verbania via Trarego, the Passo della Piazza and Premeno, but this route is only

recommended for experienced mountain drivers. The route along the shore, which continues through **Oggebbio** and **Ghiffa**, has its own wonderful panoramas, including, over on the eastern shore, the cliffs of **Rocca di Caldè** *(see page 32)*. As well as its elegant 19th-century villas and mansions, Ghiffa is well known for its traditional local manufacture of felt hats. The work of the famous hatmakers is on display at the **Museo dell'Arte del Cappello** (Corso Belvedere 279; open Apr–Oct Sat–Sun 3.30– 6.30pm), which has a collection of hats dating back to Renaissance times.

The Piedmont Shore

Verbania – Baveno – Borromean Islands – Stresa – Lake Orta – Arona (91km/56 miles)

The Piedmont shore of Lake Maggiore is the most cultural and traditional side, illustrated by its many villas and long history of famous visitors.

VERBANIA

The town of ★ **Verbania** (pop. 31,000) derives its name from the original Roman name for the lake: *Lacus Verbanus*. The two main sections of the town are Intra and ★ **Pallanza**; the former is rather industrial, while the latter is cosmopolitan, and one of the best-known resorts on the lake.

Pallanza, delightfully situated at the foot of the Monte Rosso, is separated from Intra by the Punta della Castagnola, and also by the large park surrounding the ★★ **Villa Taranto** (open end Mar–end Oct: daily 8.30am–7pm; www.villataranto.it). This park is one enormous botanical garden, containing one of the richest collections of subtropical flora in Italy, with more than 20,000 species. Rhododendrons, tulips, magnolias, dahlias, azaleas all grow here in profusion among the leaping fountains. The park originally belonged to a Scottish captain, Neil McEacharn, who bequeathed it to the Italian state on his death in 1964.

The most important structure in Pallanza itself lies north of the Borgo, on the Viale G.A. Azari: the

Star Attractions
● **Val Cannobina**
● **Villa Taranto**

Scottish outpost
In Cannobina Valley is the village of **Gurro**, whose inhabitants have Scottish ancestry. After the Battle of Pavia in 1525, a company of Scottish mercenaries fighting on the side of the French fled to this remote valley, where they settled as mountain farmers and married local women. Even today, the local dialect contains elements of Gaelic, and kilts are worn at festivals. Further Scottish influence may be found in the **Municipal Museum of Folk Costumes and Traditions** (open daily except Thur 9am–noon and 2–6pm; tel: 0323 76100), as well as in the names of establishments such as **Ristorante Scozia**.

Pallanza: blooms in Villa Taranto

Map below

Borromean Islands from Baveno

THE PIEDMONT SHORE

0   5 km

church of ★ **Madonna di Campagna**. Originally built 'in the fields', the church's beauty has been somewhat marred today by industrial buildings nearby. Built initially in the Romanesque style, the church underwent Renaissance alteration during the early 16th century. The octagonal cupola with its pillared gallery is an unusual feature, and the Romanesque campanile is also striking. Highlights inside the building include choir stalls dating from 1582, excellent 15th-century frescoes by Gerolamo Lanino, and also several 16th-century frescoes. Pallanza's **Museo del Paesaggio** (open Apr–Oct Tues–Sun 10am–noon and 3.30–6.30pm) has a fine collection of Lombard and Piedmontese art, including 16th–20th-century landscape paintings, sculptures and religious votive offerings.

Above Verbania's crowded lake promenade, the magnificent valleys and mountains are breathtakingly peaceful. The summit of the Monte Rosso (693m/2,273ft), with its view across the Gulf of Borromeo, can very nearly be reached by car along a narrow road from the Viale G.A. Azari. ★ **Monte Zeda** (2,156m/7,070ft), near Miazzina, provides an even more impressive panorama.

BAVENO

Lake Maggiore's so-called 'riviera' extends from Verbania around the Bay of Borromeo as far as Stresa. This fertile strip of land with its profusion of subtropical vegetation is best visited in early spring or late autumn when there are fewer tourists around; the views in clear weather can extend as far as the Swiss Alps.

The pinkish granite quarried near the town of ★ **Baveno** (pop. 4,500) was used in the construction of St Paul's Basilica in Rome and the Galleria Vittorio Emanuele II in Milan. Baveno's Romanesque parish church and octagonal Renaissance baptistery are worth a visit, and the town is also famous as a health spa: Crown Prince Frederick, Richard Wagner, Lord Byron and Winston Churchill all stayed here at different times.

A couple of miles north of Baveno, **Feriolo** stands on a picturesque natural bay. Once known as 'Forum Julii', the village was a station for Roman troops en route to the Alpine passes, evidence of which still exists in the ruins of watchtowers. Today it has remained true to its origins as a typical village of stonecutters and fishermen.

THE BORROMEAN ISLANDS

The promenade in Baveno provides great views of the famous ★★★ **Borromean Islands**. These four islands between Baveno, Stresa and Pallanza continue to prove irresistible to visitors. The **Isola Bella** in particular has been praised by scores of writers and poets, including Dumas and Stendhal. The Counts Borromeo were members of the same family as the Milanesi cardinals, and the first two villas to be set in extensive grounds on Lake Maggiore were on the Borromean Islands.

Of the three which you can visit, Isola Bella is the most popular. Count Carlo Borromeo III ordered it to be extravagantly crafted in the form of a ship for his wife, Isabella – hence the name Isola Bella. It is a monument to baroque theatricality, extraordinary not only for its Palazzo, but also its six shell-encrusted grottoes on the lake, and glorious

Star Attraction
● Borromean Islands

Island highlights
The **Palazzo Borromeo** (open daily mid-Mar–mid-Oct 9am–5.30pm), on Isola Bella, partly designed by Carlo Fontana, contains several majestic halls and also the famous grottoes. The terraced ★ **baroque park** is the real highlight, however, with its delightful mix of subtropical flora and white peacocks; the dream-like beauty of the whole place is marred only by all the kitsch and souvenirs on sale.

White peacock

Map
on page
26

*Below: Villa Pallavicino
gardens near Stresa
Bottom: facade in Orta*

gardens where you can strut alongside pure white peacocks. The Anfiteatro Massimo in the gardens of Isola Bella has been restored, and the full splendour of its sculptures can be admired once again.

Isola dei Pescatori (Fishermen's Island) retains some of its fishing village character with its narrow streets, but it also has some very expensive seafood restaurants. **Isola Madre** – the largest of the four islands – has some fine vegetation, including Europe's largest Kashmir cypress, and also a stylish 16th-century Palazzo Borromeo, containing interesting collections of ceramics and marionettes (open daily late Mar–late Oct 9am–5.30pm). The fourth, **Isola San Giovanni**, is privately owned.

STRESA

★ **Stresa** (pop. 4,800), one of the most elegant 19th-century resorts in Italy, is rather past its prime today. Nevertheless, many of the grand hotels still retain some of their splendour from the days when royalty, artists and aristocrats were regular visitors; Ernest Hemingway wrote his novel *Another Country* here. The Hôtel des Iles Borromées features in book IV of *A Farewell to Arms*.

The view across the lake from the *lungolago* (promenade) is highly recommended: it takes in the Borromean Islands and also the opposite shore of Lake Maggiore as far as Monte Tamaro.

LAKE ORTA

Much overshadowed by Lake Maggiore is the smaller but very beautiful ★ **Lake Orta** in Piedmont. Lago d'Orta (also called Cusio) was known to the Romans as *Lacus Cusius*, and is 13km (8 miles) long, an average of 1.5km (1 mile) wide, and measures 143m (470ft) at its deepest point. The steep Alpine ranges of Valstrona and Val d'Ossola form a spectacular contrast to the rolling green hills below.

Romantically situated on the lake is ★ **Orta San Giulio** (294m/964ft; pop. 1,130). The baroque buildings around the central piazza are charming, but the real highlight is the small ★★ **Isola di San Giulio** out in the lake, just 3 hectares (7 acres) in size, and dominated by the former episcopal palace and the ★ **Basilica di San Giulio** (open Mon–Sat 9.30am–noon and 2–6.45pm, Sun 9.30–10.45am and 2–6.45pm; Oct–Apr closes 5.30pm; Mon opens 11am). Originally founded in around 390, today's structure is predominantly Romanesque. The 12th-century black marble ★★ pulpit is still in good condition.

Another sacred site in this region is the Franciscan monastery (open daily 8.30am–6.30pm; mid-June–mid-Sept, Sat–Sun guided visits by arrangement, tel: 0322 911960; www.sacromonteorta.it) on the ★ **Sacro Monte** of Orta. There is a magnificent view from here across the western bank of Lake Orta. The outline of Madonna del Sasso, an 18th-century pilgrimage church, can be made out in the distance.

ARONA

From the southern shore of the lake it's not far to the large market town of **Arona** (pop. 14,430), with its colossal bronze ★ **statue** of its most famous son, San Carlo Borromeo, looking out across Lake Maggiore. Cardinal Borromeo (1538–84), an ardent advocate of Catholicism, was canonised in 1610; this statue of him dates from 1697, and if you go up the spiral stairway and ladder inside (open daily 8.30am–12.30pm and 2–6.30pm; winter 9am–12.30pm and 2–5pm) you

---

Star Attraction
● Isola di San Giulio

Around Stresa
There are several good excursions around Stresa. Just outside the town on the road to Arona is the ★ **Villa Pallavicino** (open Apr–Oct daily 9am–6pm) with its enormous English-style gardens. The mountainous terrain between Lake Maggiore and Lake Orta has many numbered hiking routes – and if the weather gets wet, there is the ★ **Umbrella Museum** in Gignese (open Apr–Sept Tues–Sun 10am–noon and 3–6pm). The summit of ★ **Monte Mottarone** (1,491m/4,891ft) above Stresa is a famous observation point, reached by a toll road with several hairpin bends, or by cable car from Stresa Lido.

Statue at Sacro Monte

Map
on page
18

Map on page 18

The Doll Museum

The Rocca di Angera is also home to the fascinating Museo della Bambola or Doll Museum (open Easter–Oct daily 9.30am–12.30pm and 3–7pm). This is one Europe's best doll collections, and other rooms contain children's clothes from the 17th century to the present.

Unspoiled Luino

can look out of his eyes across the lake as far as Varese *(see page 35)*. The head holds up to six people, but the steep steps make access difficult, and it is not open to children under eight years old.

At the southern end of Lake Maggiore is the industrial town of **Sesto Calende** (pop. 9,950), known to the Romans as *Sextum Calendarum*, and driven through rapidly by most people today. The region was populated very early on, however, and fascinating archaeological finds dating from the 9th century BC and earlier can be examined in the **Museo Civico** (open Tues–Sat 8.30am–12.30pm and 2.30–4.30pm, Sun 10am–noon and 3–6pm).

Sesto Calende isn't all industrial either – try visiting the ★ **Parco della Valle del Ticino**, a green oasis where the region's natural scenery is still intact. The Ticino river leaves Lake Maggiore here, and various species of bird (notably herons and swallows) nest along its banks.

The Lombardian Shore

Sesto Calende – Angera – Laveno – Luino – Maccagno – Val Veddasca (80km/50miles)

The eastern, Lombardian shore of Lake Maggiore is far removed from such noble resorts as Ascona or Stresa, and gardens and parks here are conspicuous by their absence. The eastern shore may be less spectacular, but it's far less spoilt and more rugged. The towns and small villages have so far successfully managed to escape the clutches of tourism, and are still largely owned by the local population. The hinterland is flat as far as Laveno, with several small communities dotted around, and further north the shore of the lake gets much steeper, becoming Alpine in appearance but without losing that special Mediterranean character that makes Lake Maggiore unique.

ROCCA DI ANGERA

Angera (pop. 5,560), just 8km (5 miles) from Sesto Calende *(see above)*, is a busy town situated in a pretty bay opposite Arona. The main highlight here is easily spotted: the ★ **Rocca di Angera** (open mid-Mar–late Oct Mon–Sat 9am–5.30pm; Sun and hols 9.30am–6pm), a proud fortress up on a hill behind the town, with a commanding view across the countryside and the lake.

The site is steeped in history; not far from the fortress is the cave known as the **Antro di Mitra**, where traces of the Mithraic cult (1st and 2nd centuries AD) were discovered. The castle dates back to the Torriani and the Visconti (14th century), and there are some fine ★ frescoes (1314) in the Gothic Sala della Giustizia depicting a Visconti victory. From the tower the view across to the Sacro Monte near Varese *(see page 36)* and the small island of Partegora is impressive.

SANTA CATERINA DEL SASSO

Signposts along the eastern shore of the lake, not far from the tiny village of **Reno**, point to ★★ **Santa Caterina del Sasso Ballaro** (open Easter–Oct daily 8.30am–noon and 2.30–6pm; Nov–Easter Sat–Sun 9am–noon and 2–5pm). A 12th-century chapel on the site became a Dominican monastery, which was spared destruction in the 17th century when a landslide stopped within feet of the church. The site immediately became a place of pilgrimage. In 1910, another landslide smashed through the church roof, fortunately harming no one.

Star Attraction
● **Santa Caterina del Sasso**

Below: ceiling detail of Santa Caterina del Sasso
Bottom: the monastery exterior

Map on page 18

The church and the small monastery are at their most impressive when viewed from the lake. Inside, prized frescoes include the 16th-century *Danse Macabre* in the convent's loggia. Access is by boat from April to September or by road.

LAVENO

From **Laveno** (pop. 8,900) there's a good view across the Gulf of Borromeo to the peaks of the Valais Alps. The town itself is industrial, but the local ceramic trade has a long history. In Cerro (3km/2 miles out of Laveno) the **Civica Raccolta di Terraglia museum** (open Sept–June Tues–Thur 2.30–5.30pm, Fri–Sun 10am–noon and 2.30–5.30pm; July–Aug Tues–Thur 3.30–6.30pm, Fri–Sun 10am–noon and 3.30–6.30pm; closed Mon) documents the development of this craft, introduced to the region in 1856.

Beyond Laveno is the 'Alpine' part of the eastern shore: the terrain gets steeper, and the narrow road passes through several tunnels. Soon Castelveccana comes into view, along with the famous steep rock known as the **Rocca di Caldè** (373m/1,220ft). A castle once stood on top of the rock; it was razed by Confederation troops in 1513. Just before **Porto Valtravaglia** (pop. 2,500), which lies right beside the lake, there's an interesting alternative route (with good views) via the villages of Nasca, Musadino and Muceno to **Brezzo di Bedero**. Brezza's 12th-century church of San Vittore still retains several of its Romanesque features.

LUINO

Luino (pop. 14,100) lies at the point where the valleys of the Tresa and the Travaglia meet Lake Maggiore, and is the industrial centre of the Lombardian shore. Luino's main attraction is its market, held every Wednesday since 1541. The area between the Piazza Garibaldi – graced with the first statue in Italy in honour of Giuseppe Garibaldi – and the lake promenade is filled with all manner of fascinating wares for sale.

Bucket ride

For a trip with a difference take the two seater yellow 'bucket' *(funivia)* which transports you from Laveno up to Sasso di Ferro (Rock of Iron), at 1,060m (3,480ft), just behind the town, for spectacular views over the lake. Although it may seem rather perilous the gate is fixed securely, but it is a dramatic experience nonetheless. Open daily in summer and weekends in winter.

On the Rocca di Caldè

Luino is thought to have been the birthplace of the Renaissance artist Bernadino Luini (1480–1532), but those expecting to see any works by the great painter here in Luino will be disappointed. The church of San Pietro in Campagna does have an *Adoration of the Magi* attributed to him, however. The Museo Civico in the Viale Dante contains several prehistoric finds from the region.

Hikers will enjoy the region around Luino, especially ★ **Monte Lema** (1,620m/ 5,310ft) on the border with Ticino. There are waymarked paths from Dumenza and Curiglia to the summit. Motorists can travel as far as the Rifugio Campiglio (1,184m/ 3,884ft), from which the summit is only another 1½-hour hike. In good weather, the views from up here of Lakes Lugano and Maggiore are superb.

VAL VEDDASCA

At the confluence of the Veddasca Valley lies the resort of Maccagno, separated into upper and lower sections by the Giona stream. Apart from the lake, there are numerous excursion possibilities, including the scenic ★★ **Val Veddasca**. A winding valley road leads to the almost deserted village of ★ **Indemni** just over the Swiss border, whose picturesque alleys and stone-roofed houses belie the fact that depopulation is a real problem. There are superb views on the way down to Vira.

Star Attraction
● **Val Veddasca**

Below: Luino waterfront
Bottom: Val Veddasca vernacular

Map below

Below: Arcumeggia mural
Bottom: going out in Gavirate

2: Lake Hopping

Laveno – Varese – Como (48km/29 miles)

This connecting route between Lakes Maggiore and Como has several hidden attractions: the delightful Lake Varese, for instance, surrounded by attractive rolling hills; the provincial capital of Varese, with its magnificent Sacro Monte; several fine mountain views; and Arcumeggia, a village that has become a very unusual art gallery.

ARCUMEGGIA

The first interesting detour on the route comes a few miles beyond Laveno: the little village of ★**Arcumeggia**, where contemporary Italian artists have been busy reviving the ancient art of fresco painting. There are around 170 different frescoes on the houses here, and the place is well worth a visit. This region, known as the Valcuvia, has several other attractions: the 16th-century **Villa Bozzolo** in Casalzuigno with its magnificent park, the Romanesque campanile of **San Lorenzo** in the village of Cuveglio, and a ruined Sforza fortress above Orino, on the northern slopes of the Monte Campo dei Fiori.

Travel on via Gemonio (Romanesque church with frescoes) to **Gavirate** (pop. 9,400), the main town picturesquely situated on the northern shore

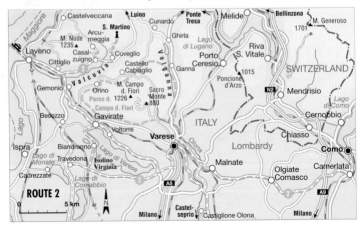

ROUTE 2

of **Lake Varese**. This 8-km (5-mile) long lake measures 4km (2 miles) at its widest point, and is very shallow (max depth 26m/85ft); its banks are thus rather marshy and this has spared it much new building construction. Vineyards cloak the hills at the foot of **Monte Campo dei Fiori** (1,226m/ 4,020ft), and also south of the lake.

VOLTORRE

There are several fine cultural sights in the Lake Varese region, especially in **Voltorre** (2km/ 1½ miles from Gavirate), where the parish church of **San Michele** has a superb 12th-century Romanesque ★ cloister, and also the church of **Santa Maria della Neve** in **Travedona** (7km/ 4 miles southwest of Gavirate on Lake Monate).

VARESE

The provincial capital of Varese (pop. 83,830) was still quite insignificant during the Middle Ages, but has now developed into a typically Northern Italian metropolis with a lot of industry – and industrial pollution, though great efforts have been made to clean it up. Varese is known as 'the city of gardens and shoes' for its shoe making and its abundance of old villas and parks. The city lies in the region known as the Varesotto, which extends from Lake Lugano up to the edge of Greater Milan, and includes the famous Sacro Monte, Castiglione Olona and Castelseprio.

One of the most noticeable features of the town is the baroque campanile (77m/252ft) of the basilica of **San Vittore**, built between 1580 and 1615; the original Renaissance structure was given a neoclassical facade in 1788. The building contains frescoes by leading Lombard masters, and the neighbouring ★ **baptistery** has several fresco fragments dating from the 13th and 14th centuries.

The old part of Varese is centred around San Vittore, but there's a sharp contrast just a short distance away in the Piazza Monte Grappa, where buildings from 1927 to 1935 all bear the unmistakeable stamp of Italian Fascist architecture. Inside the Villa

> **Neighbouring lakes**
> To the southwest of lake Varese are two smaller lakes: Lake **Comabbio** and Lake **Monate**. A third one, Lake Biandronno, is almost completely dry now. A number of remains of prehistoric lake dwellings have been discovered in this region, and some of the finds can be seen in the **Museo Preistorico** (open Apr–Oct Sat–Sun 2–6pm) on the tiny island of Virginia in Lake Varese.
>
> As well as offering the museum, **Isolina Virginia** is the perfect spot for a picnic or lunch in its little restaurant. Boats depart from Biandronno on Lake Varese's western shore.

Palazzo Estense in Varese

Map on page 34

Below: the Way of the Cross at Sacro Monte
Bottom: inside Santa Maria del Monte

Mirabello, the **Municipal Museum** (open Tues–Sat 10.30am–12.30pm and 2.30–6.30pm, Sun 9.30am–12.30pm and 2–5pm) has interesting prehistoric exhibits and an art gallery. Its Roman finds include the "bambino di Varese" (child of Varese), one of Italy's best-preserved mummies.

On the hillside of Biumo Superiore, north of the city, lies one of the region's most important contemporary art galleries. The ★★ **Villa Panza** (open Feb–mid-Dec Tues–Sun 10am–6pm; www.fondoambiente.it) is set among splendid gardens. Inside there is a superb collection of mainly American art from the 1980s and 90s as well as rich 16th–19th century furnishings, an important collection of African and pre-Columbian art, and many works by New York artist Dan Flavin.

SACRO MONTE

A good excursion is to the ★ **Sacro Monte** (880m/2,880ft) or 'Holy Mountain', a famous place of pilgrimage. A pilgrimage church was built on the mountain in the 10th century, and it was later used to house a statue of the Virgin, known as the Black Madonna because it is carved from dark wood. In the 16th century, plans were drawn up for a ★ **Via Crucis** (Way of the Cross), lined with chapels. Thanks to the skills of the architect Giuseppe Bernascone, who built the round domed

structures at the beginning of the 17th century, the ascent along the cobbled 2-km (1½-mile) route, leading from the Prima Cappella to the church of Santa Maria del Monte, is unforgettable. Art and landscape combine harmoniously; the chapels are decorated with many frescoes and several larger-than-life terracotta figures. The church of **Santa Maria del Monte**, in which the 14th-century Black Madonna still stands, is a mixture of styles from Romanesque to baroque; its massive campanile is particularly striking, and the early 11th-century crypt contains some fine Gothic frescoes.

CASTIGLIONE OLONA

While in Varese, travel 8km (5 miles) southwards to ★★**Castiglione Olona** (churches and museum open Apr–Sept Tues–Sat 9am–noon and 3–6pm, Sun 10am–12.30pm and 3–6pm; Oct–Mar closed Sun am), which today is a small and rather insignificant industrial town. During the Renaissance, however, it was turned into a kind of 'mini-Florence' in the middle of Lombardy by Cardinal Branda Castiglione (1350–1443).

The numerous palazzi of Castiglione Olona, including that of the cardinal himself, have lost much of their former glory, but the sacred buildings are still magnificent. The ★**Chiesa di Villa** (1422–43) is reminiscent of Brunelleschi's work in Florence, and the ★**Collegiata** (open Oct–Mar Tues–Sun 10am–noon and 2.30–5pm; Apr–Sept Tues–Sun 9.30am–noon and 3–6pm), reached by an idyllic walk, contains marvellous frescoes by the Florentine artist Masolino da Panicale (1435), who also painted the *Scenes from the Life of John the Baptist* in the ★baptistery.

TRANSPORT MUSEUM

To reach Lake Como from Varese, take the SS 342 via Malnate and Olgiate-Comasco. The most common type of building along this route is unfortunately the *supermercato*, but there's an interesting coach, steam train and bicycle museum in the Villa Rachele-Ogliari in **Malnate**.

Star Attractions
- Castiglione Olona
  - Villa Panza

Local archaeology
Not far from Castiglione Olona, the excavation site to the east of the small village of ★ **Castelseprio** was probably a settlement founded by the Celtic Insubrians, then the capital of a Lombard province, and then a powerful medieval commune, before its destruction by the Visconti in 1287. Several ruined walls have been exposed to view.

The small church of **Santa Maria Foris Portas** nearby probably dates from the 7th century originally, and contains a magnificent ★ fresco cycle which, though incomplete, was painted sometime between the 7th and 9th centuries. It, too, is part of the Zona Archeologica (open Tues–Sat 8.30am–7.30pm, Sun 9.30am–6.30pm, reduced hours in winter).

Castiglione Olona

Map
on page
39

3: Lake Lugano

Lake Lugano is 271m (889ft) above sea-level, and measures 48.9sq km (19sq miles); three-quarters of the lake lie in Ticino. With its strange shape and steep, rocky shores, Lake Lugano is reminiscent of Lake Lucerne minus the Alpine backdrop.

Changing perspectives
The best view of the lake, which has an average width of less than 2km (1½ miles), can be had from the hills around Lugano, but for a proper experience of the *Cere-sio*, as the locals refer to their lake, take a boat trip past the rocky mountain slopes. Unlike Lakes Como or Maggiore, the large amount of weed in Lake Lugano means that its dark-green water never appears transparent, even on sunny days.

*Below: Lake Lugano from a
Swiss perspective*
*Bottom: detail on Lugano's
Piazza della Riforma*

Lugano to Como

Lugano – Melide – Morcote – Bissone – Riva San Vitale – Mendrisio (32km/20 miles)

★★**Lugano** (pop. 26,100), the largest city in Ticino, is magnificently situated in its semicircular bay, between the peaks of **Monte Brè** (925m/ 3,034ft) in the east and **Monte Salvatore** (912m/2,992ft) in the south. The wonderful mixture of stunning mountain scenery and mild, sunny climate has made the region around Lugano one of the most popular tourist areas in Switzerland, although the sheer speed of construction work over the past few decades has also resulted in a fair amount of insensitive building and 'development'. Lugano is famous for its warm microclimate, and Monte Brè is known as Switzerland's sunniest mountain. Funiculars run to the summits of both Monte Brè and San Salvatore, departing every 30 minutes from Lugano.

Archaeological finds date the earliest settlement of the region back to pre-Roman times. The city received its first written mention (as *Luano*) in AD818. During the Middle Ages Lugano was often involved in the struggles between Milan and Como. From 1803 to 1978 it alternated as the capital of Ticino with Bellinzona and Locarno.

CITY TOUR

The best place to start any tour of the city is the **Piazza della Riforma**, with its elegant 19th-century buildings. The cafés here are popular meeting-places for young and old alike. The **Municipio**, or Town Hall, on the south side of the piazza, dates from 1844, and the famous lake promenades lead southwards and eastwards towards Paradiso and the municipal park.

Inland is the largely traffic-free city centre, where several old buildings still survive. The Via Pessina has picturesque arcades and typical cobblestones, and the Via Nassa, which joins it to the south, has now become the city's main shopping street. It comes out in the Piazza B. Luini, named after the Milanese Renaissance painter Bernaldo Luini, several of whose works can be admired here in the church of ★★ **Santa Maria degli Angioli**. Built in 1515, the church belonged to a Franciscan monastery that was dissolved in 1848. The interior is dominated by Luini's enormous *Crucifixion*, which he completed in 1529 while under the influence of Leonardo da Vinci. Three other frescoes – the *Last Supper* on the south wall, and the *Mourning of Christ* and *Mary with Jesus and St John* – were originally painted by Luini for the monastery.

Just along the waterfront from Santa Maria degli Angioli is the **Museum of Modern Art** (Museo d'Arte Moderna), Riva Antonio Caccia, 5 (open Tues–Fri 10am–noon and 2–6pm,

Star Attraction
● **Santa Maria degli Angioli**

Santa Maria degli Angioli

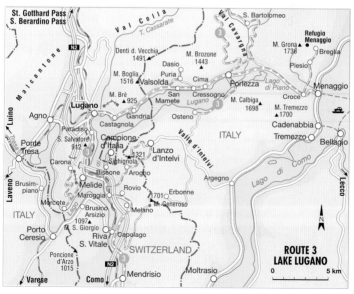

ROUTE 3
LAKE LUGANO

0   5 km

Map on page 39

Sat–Sun 11am–6pm), which has a good pro-
gramme of visiting temporary exhibitions.

THE CATHEDRAL

High above the old town is the ★ **Cathedral of
San Lorenzo**. First mentioned as a parish church
in 818, it dates back to an old Roman pillared
basilica that was vaulted and extended in the 13th
century, before receiving its side chapels in the
18th century and much interior renovation. The
★ Renaissance facade (1500–17) is very attractive, with its three portals, richly carved figures
and round window, and is considered one of the
finest examples of Lombard Renaissance architecture in Ticino.

Below: café life in Lugano
Below: Villa Favorita

Don't miss the city's museums either, espe-
cially the **Museo Cantonale d'Arte** (Palazzo
Reali, Via Canova 10, open Wed–Sun 10am–
5pm, Tues 2–5pm) and the Museo Cantonale di
Storia Naturale. The **Villa Favorita**, Strada
Castagnola, Via Rivera 14, in Castagnola (Easter–
Oct Fri–Sun 10am–5pm) contains an important
display of 19th- and 20th-century American and
European works of art in oils and watercolours.

The **Museo Civico di Belle Arti** (open
Tues–Sun 10am–noon, 2–6pm) is the most important collection of Ticinese art, housed in the elegant Villa Ciani. There are 4,000 works by both

Swiss and foreign artists from the 13th to the 20th centuries, including examples by Monet, Matisse and Rousseau. The gardens also have a splendid collection of subtropical trees.

MORCOTE

Melide is a popular holiday resort with a special attraction: the 1:25 scale models collectively known as ★ **Swissminiatur** (open daily Mar–Nov 9am–5pm; July–Aug 9am–10pm), representing the most important towns, buildings and means of transport of Switzerland.

A cable railway leads up from the lake to ★ **Carona**, a picturesque mountain village with several attractive churches. From here it's possible to hike along the mountain to the next destination on the route, the delightful village of ★★ **Morcote**. Even though it was discovered by the tourist industry quite early on, Morcote has successfully retained much of its historic substance. The village blends in harmoniously with its surroundings, and this has made it a magnet for visitors. A flight of steep steps laid out in 1732 leads up to the terraced cemetery and parish church of ★ **Santa Maria del Sasso**, built in the 13th century; inside there are several Renaissance frescoes. The free-standing campanile dates from 1539. From here there are magnificent views.

Near the village of **Bissone** is the Ponte Diga, built in 1844, which takes rail and road traffic across the narrowest part of the lake.

> **Famous inhabitants**
> **Bissone** is famous as the home of several well-known families of artists, such as Borromini, Maderno and Tencalla. Its most revered son was the architect Francesco Borromini (1599–1667), the biggest rival of Gian Lorenzo Bernini in Rome. Bissone does not possess even one of the master's works, however.

Morcote

LITERARY EXCURSION

An excursion to the small village of **Montagnola** will reward lovers of the works of German writer Herman Hesse, who became a Swiss citizen.

The **Herman Hesse Museum** (open Mar–Oct daily 10am–6.30pm; Nov–Feb Sat–Sun 10am–5.30pm) displays his final home, the Casa Rossa, where he wrote *Steppenwolf*, *Siddhartha* and *Narcissus and Goldmund*. His paintings and poetry are also on display as well as his glasses and straw hat. Just north of Montagnola is Gentilino, the site of his grave.

Map
on page
39

Capolago

At the southern end of Lake Lugano is **Capolago**. Fortified by the Visconti, it was an important trading centre before the Gotthard railway was built. It is the birthplace of architect Carlo Maderna (1556–1629), who built the facade of St Peter's in Rome. Capolago is the starting point for tours to ★★ **Monte Generoso** (1,701m/5,580ft); in good weather the panorama from the summit extends from Monte Viso (3,841m/12,600ft) to the Bernina (4,049m/13,280ft). Early summer, when the flowers are in bloom, is the best time to take the rack railway to the top.

RIVA SAN VITALE

The small town of **Riva San Vitale** (pop. 2,000) is most famous for its Early Christian baptistery and the domed church of Santa Croce. Inhabited as long ago as prehistoric times, and first mentioned as *Sobenno* in 774, during medieval times Riva San Vitale was one of Como's bases in its war against Milan. The town is dominated by the mighty dome of ★★ **Santa Croce**, one of the finest churches in Switzerland. It was built between 1588 and 1592 by the architect Giovanni Antonio Piotto, from Vacallo in the Mendrisiotto. Despite sharing some characteristics with contemporary centralised structures (e.g. Todi, Montepulciano), the building also presages the baroque era. Eight mighty columns support the huge dome crowned with its lantern. The fresco decoration, with its many strange figures and gargoyle-like Mannerist faces, is also very impressive.

In protest at new boundaries, the villagers of Riva San Vitale declared themselves an independent republic in 1798. They held out for 14 days before being persuaded to rejoin Switzerland.

BAPTISTERY OF SAN GIOVANNI

Baptistery of San Giovanni

Riva San Vitale's second claim to fame is its ★★ **Baptistery of San Giovanni**, beside the parish church of San Vitale. The centralised structure, with its octagonal cupola, was built in around 500, and originally had a square ambulatory (some parts of the original roof still survive in the western wall). The eastern apse probably dates from the Carolingian period; the fresco remains showing the *Crucifixion* have been dated to around 1000; and the paintings in the niches to the left and right of the apse date from the 14th and 15th centuries. Some sections of the artistically paved marble floor also survive; the octagonal *piscina* in the pavement was originally used for total-immersion baptisms before the erection of the enormous baptism stone (2m/7ft across).

The municipal museum in Riva also contains an interesting exhibition of works by the 19th-century 'mountain painter' Giovanni Segantini.

MENDRISIO

From Riva, continue to **Mendrisio** (pop. 6,200), a lively town which has retained its *borgo* (old town), several churches and numerous palazzi, despite a lot of new construction. The colourful Easter processions here are famous. The old town centre is dominated by the parish church of **SS Cosma e Damiano**, a monumental structure dating from the 19th century with an octagonal dome. The former monastery church of San Giovanni Battista was built above a previous structure between 1722 and 1738; it contains some marvellous stucco and several *trompe l'oeil* ceiling paintings. Mendrisio also possesses one of the most magnificent baroque palazzi in Ticino: the **Palazzo Pollini** (1719–21). Mendriso is in a wine-producing area and is a good base from which to visit the surrounding vineyards.

Lugano to Menaggio

Lugano – Gandria –Porlezza – Menaggio (28km/17 miles)

This route leads from Lugano, via the very picturesque village of Gandria, to Menaggio on Lake Como. The itinerary covers regions that are not only very scenic but have also produced several fine artists and architects over the centuries.

Star Attractions
- **Monte Generoso panorama**
- **Santa Croce**
- **Baptistery of San Giovanni**

Below and Bottom: Church of SS Cosma e Damiano in Mendrisio

Map
on page
39

GANDRIA

Leave Lugano along the road to Porlezza, which
follows a steep section beyond Castagnola, with
fine views across the lake and the Sighignola
Massif. Along this section of road it's actually
quite easy to miss ★ **Gandria** (7km/4 miles east
of Lugano), which lies just below the route. This
much-visited village is a jumble of houses on a
steep slope right beside the lake, and is very pretty,
especially when viewed from the water. It can
be reached on foot from Castagnola (1hr), along
a path lined with subtropical vegetation.

On the opposite bank is the Cantine di Gandria landing stage. Here the original **Museo
Doganale Svizzero** or Customs Museum (open
Apr–mid-Oct daily 1.30–5.30pm) is worth a brief
visit; it contains a fascinating selection of ingen-
iously smuggled goods and 'catch the smuggler'
computer games for children.

Below: Gandria promenade
Bottom: dining high above
the lake, in Sighignola

VALSOLDA

Beyond Gandria the route crosses the Italian border. The hamlet of San Mamete marks the entrance
to the picturesque ★ **Valsolda**, a long valley surrounded by high Dolomite peaks which is very
popular with hikers and climbers. The small village of **Puria** was the birthplace of one of the most
important artist-architects of the Lombard Renais-

sance, Pellegrino Tibaldi (1527–96). He worked in this region and also in Rome and Milan, but his career took off properly when he worked for Philip II in Madrid. Valsolda was also home the author Antonio Fogazzaro (1842–1911), who set his novel *Piccolo Mondo Antico* in this region.

The mountains and the lake provide an atmospheric backdrop for the ★**Santuario della Madonna della Caravina**, a magnificent baroque structure built in 1663, situated above the main road between Cressogno and Cima.

PORLEZZA

The town of **Porlezza** (pop. 4,184) marks the eastern end of Lake Lugano. It dates back to prehistoric times, and during the Roman era was the port of *Raetia*. Later on this fishing town, like so many others between Lakes Maggiore and Como, was the home of several generations of artists, including the Sanmichele and Della Porta families. Guglielmo della Porta was a pupil of Michelangelo, and is famous for his work on the dome of St Peter's in Rome after his master's death in 1564.

Unfortunately Porlezza has no important artistic monuments of its own. The parish church of **San Vittore** (17th-century with fresco decoration) is worth a visit, as is the Romanesque campanile of the ruined church of San Maurizio, outside the town at the foot of the Monte Calbiga (1,698m/5,570ft). The church marks the site of the former Porlezza, which was destroyed in a landslide. Remains of an early medieval settlement have been discovered.

ALPINE VALLEYS

Not far away from Porlezza is the ★**Val Cavargna**, a beautiful mountain region with several pretty villages, magnificent chestnut groves and beech forests, a profusion of wild flowers and numerous walking and hiking routes. One well-surfaced route connects Porlezza with both the Val Cavargna and the **Val Rezzo**, and a 30-km (18-mile) round trip by car affords several

Porlezza excursions
There are several good excursions from Porlezza. Try visiting **Osteno** on the southern shore of Lake Lugano, with its attractive church; inside there is an astounding marble ★ *Madonna and Child* by Andrea Bregno, dated 1464. Halfway between Porlezza and Osteno the road leads past the entrance to the **Grotte di Rescia**, a small limestone cavern.

Porlezza local

Map on page 39

Recommended view
One particularly good view of the lake and its mountain backdrop can be enjoyed from the **Crocetta a Specchi** (505m/ 1,650ft), easily and quickly reached from **Croce**; it takes around an hour to climb the **Sasso di San Martino** (862m/2,820ft), where a magnificent panorama meets the eye, extending northeast as far as the granite peaks of the Bergell.

Below: mountain and lake view
Bottom: Menaggio fishmonger

magnificent views of the region. Note the abandoned mountain hamlets, however: the problem of depopulation affects many of these Southern Alpine valleys.

Several more marked routes lead from Buggiolo (1,035m/3,400ft) to the Passo di San Lucio (1,548m/5,075ft; 2hrs), an ancient way of gaining access to the Val Colla in Ticino, and along the ridge of the Monte Garzirola (2,116m/6,940ft; 2hrs from San Lucio), which is famed for its magnificent panoramic views.

MOUNTAIN VIEWS

The road to Menaggio leads past the small and shallow Lago di Piano, which has a maximum depth of around 5m (16ft) and was once a part of Lake Lugano. Towering above the vineyards of Carlazzo here is the high rocky peak of **Monte Grona** (1,736m/5,695ft), and across to the right is the forest-covered northern flank of **Monte Tremezzo** (1,700m/5,580ft).

At the tiny hamlet of **Croce**, the road begins its winding descent to the western bank of Lake Como, with some good views of Bellagio and the mountains around the Valsassina.

MENAGGIO

The busy little town of **Menaggio** (pop. 3,000) lies on a small promontory at the point where the Val Sanagra meets Lake Como. Besides its very good beach, Menaggio has many bars, restaurants and shops around the central piazza, but is also where the main road to Lugano branches off, resulting in heavy traffic, particularly in the summer. The area slightly inland is far more peaceful.

A winding road leads north to Plesio and on to **Breglia**, with its little Madonna di Breglia church, and also the observation point known as the Belvedere San Domenico (820m/2,690ft). From Breglia, hikers can follow the path to the **Rifugio Menaggio** (with superb views of Lake Como) and from there continue to the summit of Monte Grona.

4: The City of Como

The city of **Como** (pop. 83,000) has two distinct faces: one historic, facing the lake, and one industrial, which extends into the Brianza. Como is best approached from the north, either across the lake or along one of the lakeside roads, when the town is at its most magical: green, grey and a soft ochre. Bathed in golden sunlight, the walls of the old town retain a sobriety that is distinctly Lombard.

Map below

Cathedral carving in Como

The first craftsmen to make the town famous were the master architects and stonemasons from the region, known as *Maestri Comacini*; the town's industrial future was assured by the introduction of silk manufacturing in 1510 by Pietro Boldoni. *Pura seta di Como* (pure Como silk) is a phrase often heard, since Como is Italy's top producer of silk, though the raw fibre comes from East Asia.

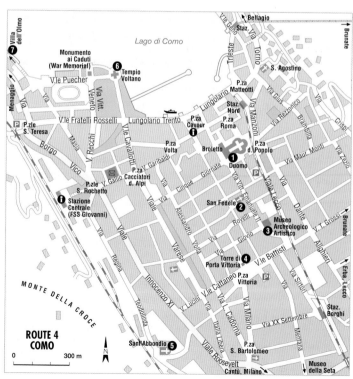

ROUTE 4
COMO

0   300 m

Map on page 47

Below: Como street scene
Bottom: family outing

HISTORY

Though inhabited long before the Romans arrived, Como is most famous historically as the birthplace of Pliny the Elder (AD24–79), compiler of the 37-volume *Naturalis Historia*, and of his nephew Pliny the Younger (AD62–113). The Romans were followed by Lombards and Franks, and during the Middle Ages Como suffered from several battles between the Guelphs (pro-papacy) and the Ghibellines (pro-empire). As an independent commune from the 11th to the 14th century, it was home to a famous school of master builders, architects and sculptors (*Maestri Comacini*) whose work is still much admired.

During the Ten Years' War with Milan (1118–27), the town was partially destroyed, but managed to recover largely because of support from the emperor Barbarossa. From 1335 Como was ruled by the Visconti, and from 1450 by the Sforza, and flourished culturally as a result – only to decline under Spanish rule, which lasted until 1714. Economic recovery only really began under the Austrian Habsburgs, and the silk industry in particular made Como quite prosperous again.

Today the old town of Como – the *città murata* – is largely closed to motor traffic, and its layout is almost identical to that of the original Roman *castrum* on the site. For some time now there has been a complete ban on new

construction; restoration is the order of the day. Como's ancient walls and arcades are ideal for a stroll back into the centuries, and the gourmet specialities and exclusive fashions make shopping here a very memorable experience.

Star Attraction
● **Duomo**

CITY TOUR

The best place to start a tour of the historic old town is the cathedral square, Piazza Duomo, in which the ★★ **Duomo** ❶ (Cathedral; open daily 7am–noon and 3–7pm), the **Broletto** (former town hall, built in 1215) and the **Torre del Comune** (old city tower) form a harmonious and grandiose architectural ensemble. Both the Torre del Comune and the Broletto, with its Tuscan-style black-and-white patterned facade, date from the early 13th century; the cathedral was begun somewhat later, in 1396, and construction work continued – with the odd interruption – right into the 18th century. Nevertheless, the building as a whole is exceptionally harmonious and it is one of Italy's finest examples of Gothic-Renaissance style. The 75-m (245-ft) high dome above the crossing was built in 1744 by the Turin architect Juvara.

Lorenzo degli Spagli's original design was Gothic; the ★ facade, begun in 1457, is considered a masterpiece of Early Lombard Renaissance architecture. Much of its statuary is by the Rodari brothers, such as the *Adoration of the Magi* relief in the lunette, and the two seated figures, Pliny the Elder and Pliny the Younger, placed proudly on either side of the main portal. Tommaso and Jacopo Rodari also did the so-called Porta della Rana or 'Frog Portal' on the northern side of the cathedral, which owes its name to a rather sketchy relief of a frog.

The interior of the cathedral is rather dark, but it contains several artistic masterpieces including the enormous 16th-century Tuscan and Flemish tapestries lining the nave, a fine *Deposition* by Tommaso Rodari in the left transept, and several altar paintings by the great Bernardino Luini (*Adoration of the Magi*) and Gaudenzio Ferrari (*Flight from Egypt*).

Como admirers
Of all the lakes, Como is perhaps the most romantic and voluptuously Italian. It has inspired countless writers, poets and musicians since the days of the early Roman Empire. These days, the Italian lakes are awash with fashion designers, footballers and film stars. George Clooney has a lakeside villa, George Lucas filmed parts of *Star Wars II* in the area and Donatella Versace throws A-list parties at her mansion. The celebrity glitz is centred around Como and Bellagio – the 'Comowood' of the lakes.

Cathedral interior

Map
on page
47

SAN FEDELE

Just a few short steps away from the cathedral is the church of ★ **San Fedele** ➋ (open daily 8am–noon and 3.30–7pm), a 10th–12th-century Romanesque basilica, built by the *Maestri Comacini*, on the ruins of an earlier Carolingian structure – Como's original cathedral. The apse, with its dwarf gallery, and the trefoil ground-plan are both reminiscent of Charlemagne's Palatine Chapel in Aachen. The northern portal has some very fine sculpture work, and inside to the left of the northern apse there are several frescoes dating from the 12th and 13th centuries, thematically related to the ones in the baptistery of Riva San Vitale *(see page 42)*.

Silk museum
Although silkworms are no longer raised here, Chinese silk thread is dyed and woven around Como, making it Italy's largest producer of silk. The **Silk Museum**, Museo Didattico della Seta, is south of the centre at Via Castelnuovo 9 (open Tues–Fri 9am–noon and 3–6pm; tel: 031 303180) where the Silk-makers' School gives a fascinating insight into the craft.

Below: museum vase
Bottom: Lombard painting
in the gallery

SANT'ABBONDIO

The Palazzo Giovio houses the ★ **Museo Archeologico Artistico** ➌ (open Tues–Sat 9.30am–12.30pm, 2–5pm, Sun 10am–1pm), one of Como's two municipal museums. The oldest finds here date from around 8000BC, and there are also several Roman, Romanesque and Gothic exhibits. The **picture gallery** documents Lombard art of the 16th to 18th centuries, and there is also a section displaying art from the various Mediterranean cultures.

The other museum, the **Museo del Risorgimento G. Garibaldi** (open Tues–Sat 9.30am–12.30pm and 2–5pm, Sun 10am–1pm), inside the Palazzo Olginati next door to the Palazzo Giovio, has some interesting exhibits documenting the town's history, its 19th-century liberation struggles and the two World Wars.

One of the most majestic gates still surviving from Como's medieval fortifications is the mighty **Torre di Porta Vittoria** ➍, a full 40m (130ft) high, with its oversized double windows.

From the Piazza Vittoria it's not far to the church of ★★ **Sant'Abbondio** ➎ (open daily 7am–6pm), another example of *Maestri Comacini* architecture, and one of the most important Early Lombard Romanesque structures in Italy, now lying between the railway and an industrial site. The five-aisled basilica, with its two bell-towers, has several stylistic features in common with structures north of the Alps (e.g. Speyer Cathedral in Germany). The strikingly large choir contains Gothic frescoes dating from around 1350. The ★ **cloister** to the north of the building, with its twin-storeyed arcade, was added in the 16th century.

Star Attraction
● Sant'Abbondio

TO THE WEST

There's a good view of the town and the lake from the **Castello Baradello** (access via the Piazza San Rocco) 3km/2 miles south of Como, an enchanting ruined fort on the eastern slopes of the Monte della Croce (536m/1,760ft). Out on the western side of the harbour is the neoclassical structure known as the **Tempio Voltiano** ❻ (open Apr–Sept Tues–Sun 10am–noon and 3–6pm; Oct–Mar 10am–noon and 2–4pm), dedicated to the famous physicist and discoverer Alessandro Volta (1745–1827), after whom the electrical unit volt is named; his personal effects and also the batteries he invented are on display here.

The western lake promenade leads from Piazza Cavour past several attractive neoclassical villas to the ★ **Villa dell'Olmo** ❼ (open Mon–Sat 8am–6pm), an estate laid out in 1782–87. Its first important visitors were Napoleon and Josephine, who arrived just after the building was completed. The Villa dell'Olmo is the most majestic of the neoclassical villas in this part of Como.

Below: frescoed facade
Bottom: youth hostel at Villa dell'Olmo

Map
below

5: Lake Como

Over the centuries the splendid countryside around Lake Como has tempted people to add their own piece of beauty, and it is probably true to say that this lake, known to the Romans as *Lacus Lario*, is the most impressive of the Upper Italian lakes. Not only Como Cathedral, but also the rows of magnificent villas with beautiful gardens along the edge of the lake, all testify to the harmonious

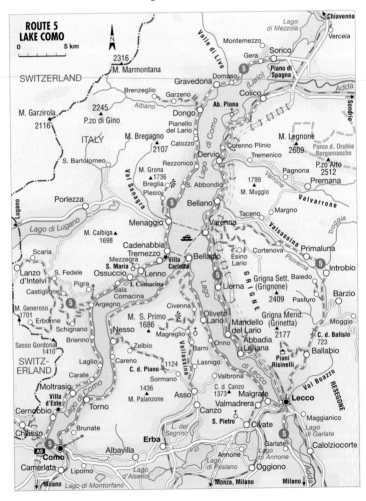

blend of natural scenery and architecture in this part of the world. Like a fjord, Lake Como is surrounded by steep mountains. Unlike Lake Maggiore, it does not extend across a plain; it is an Alpine lake, despite its Mediterranean vegetation, and southern-baroque style villas and parks.

But this contrast is what makes the Lario, as it is called locally, so attractive. Even though its surface area of 146sq km (56sq miles) makes it only the third-largest lake in Upper Italy, with its depth of 410m (1,345ft) it is the deepest inland lake in southern Europe. Lake Como, roughly 50km (32 miles) long and 4.5km (3 miles) across at its widest point, is shaped a little like an upside-down 'Y'. The rivers flowing in are the Mera, which descends from the Bergell, and the Adda, from Bernina Massif, which leaves the lake near Lecco, finally joining the Po not far from Cremona.

Star Attraction
● **Intelvi Valley**

Popular retreat
Como is a popular retreat for the city dwellers of Milan, less than an hour's drive away. Try to avoid driving at peak times on Friday afternoon/evening and Sunday afternoon when the whole world seems to be heading to the lake.

Below: sunbathing by the lake
Bottom: guests at Villa d' Este

The Western Shore

Cernobbio – Tremezzo – Menaggio – Gravedona – Sorico (59km/37 miles)

The route up the lake from Como first arrives at **Cernobbio** (pop. 7,000), where the **Villa d'Este** begins the long line of famous residences along the lake's western shore. Built between 1565–70 by Pellegrino Tibaldi, the villa was altered in the early 19th century by Caroline of Brunswick, the estranged wife of Britain's Prince Regent, in accordance with contemporary taste. Today the Villa d'Este is a luxury hotel and open only to guests, apart from the (very expensive) La Veranda restaurant.

Pass gardens and villas to reach **Carate**, where the small 11th-century church of Santa Maria is just a short distance above the main road. The Romanesque campanile, 15th-century frescoes and view of the lake form a memorable ensemble.

INTELVI VALLEY

The small town of **Argegno** is a good starting-point for a detour into the ★★ **Intelvi Valley**, a

Map
on page
52

*Below: parish church at
Scaria in the Intelvi Valley
Bottom: coffee ceremony on
Isola Comacina*

high plateau with some delightful landscape, but famed above all for producing a whole host of painters, architects and stonemasons.

The *Maestri Antelami* not only influenced Lombard art for decades but were active all over Europe and even the Near East. Several of them *(see box on page 55)* have also left their mark in the Valle d'Intelvi: in **Scaria**, for instance, which has superb stucco work by Diego Carlone and fine frescoes by Carlo Carlone in the 13th-century church Santi Nazaro Ecelso. There are also other artistic and architectural discoveries to be made.

The Valle d'Intelvi is wonderful for walkers too, and its location between Lake Lugano and Lake Como provides a whole series of magnificent panoramic views to accompany hikes. One particularly impressive peak for climbers to head for here is the **Sassa Gordona** (1,410m/4,625ft).

ISOLA COMACINA

Just before Sala Comacina, the only island in Lake Como comes into view: **Isola Comacina**. Around 600m (640yds) long and up to 200m (220yds) wide, the island was settled during Roman times, and during the Middle Ages there were five churches on it at one point. In 1169 the settlement was wiped out by Como in retaliation for its pact with Milan during the Ten Years' War (1118–27).

All that remains today of the original town are the ruined walls of the Romanesque basilica of Sant'Eufemia. The main reason to visit the island (reached by ferry) is to have lunch at the lakeside Locanda dell'Isola Comacina (tel: 0344 55083/56755).

Isola Comacina is famous for its festivities and fireworks around 24 June, St John the Baptist's Day. The celebrations feature a parade of boats illuminated by thousands of twinkling *lumaghitti* – snail shells made into little oil lamps (*see also Festivals page 108*).

Facing Isola Comacina is **Villa del Balbianello** (gardens open Apr–Oct 10am–12.30pm and 3.30–6.30pm, closed Mon and Wed; tel: 0344 56110; accessible by boat on weekdays, at weekends access by foot from Lenno). This utterly photogenic villa, built in the 18th century by Cardinal Duini over the ruins of a medieval monastery, featured in the fifth 'Star Wars' instalment, *Attack of the Clones*, in 2002. Villa Balbianello also starred in the 2006 version of *Casino Royale* as the sanatorium where Bond (played by Daniel Craig) recovers after his nasty encounter with a knotted rope. Business is now booming.

OSSUCCIO AND LENNO

At the entrance to the Val Perlana is **Ossuccio** (pop. 1,500), where the simple church of Santa Maria Maddalena has an unusual campanile with a brick belfry, dating from the 14th century. Above the village is a 17th-century *Via Crucis* (a symbolic representation of the path taken by Christ on the way to his crucifiction) with 14 chapels, and higher still, the basilica of ★★ **San Benedetto** in the Val Perlana – probably the finest of the Romanesque churches on the lake.

Lenno also has an interesting church: **Santo Stefano** (open daily 8am–noon and 3–6pm), though much renovated during the 16th century, is originally Lombard. The crypt was part of an 11th-century basilica, and remains of a Roman bath have been discovered beneath the church. The octagonal baptistery is also 11th-century.

Star Attraction
● **San Benedetto**

Maestri Antelami

The *Maestri Antelami* are so called after the 12th-century sculptor and architect, Benedetto Antelami. Famous for his design of Parma's exquisite pink marble octagonal Baptistery, he was born in the Val d'Intelvi, which in the Middle Ages was actually known as the Val Antelami because of its famous son. Antelami inspired the most superb of masons and master builders, creating a dynasty of excellence. At the height of their fame as late as the 18th century, they were employed in the courts of Russia, Austria, Naples and Spain.

Ossuccio fisherman

Map on page 52

Villa Carlotta
The two lakeside resorts of ★ **Tremezzo** and **Cadenabbia** are almost always busy, especially in the area round the ★★★ **Villa Carlotta** (open daily Apr–Sept 9am–6pm; Mar and Oct 9–11.30am and 2–4.30pm; closed Nov–Feb), the most famous and the most lavishly decorative villa on Lake Como. Its terraced gardens, elegant rooms, sculpture and painting collection and fine views attract many visitors. Originally built in the baroque style (1747), the present neoclassical appearance dates from the beginning of the 19th century. Sold to Princess Mary of Prussia in 1856, it was bequeathed to her daughter Charlotte, known as Carlotta.

Just inland from Lenno, **Mezzegra** comes into view. The place is famous for one reason: it was here on 28 April 1945, one day after having been taken prisoner in nearby Dongo while trying to flee to Switzerland, that Benito Mussolini and his mistress Clara Petacci were shot dead.

MENAGGIO

The route now continues on to **Menaggio** (*see page 46*), beyond which the landscape gradually begins to get starker, and generally more Alpine than Mediterranean. Snowy mountain peaks start appearing; the northern end of the Lario is only around 40km (24 miles) away from the main Alpine range. The lakeshore road leads through Sant'Abbondio, Rezzonico and the collection of communities making up Pianello del Lario. There's a good ★ **boat museum** (Museo della Barca Lariana, open daily July–Sept 2.30–6pm; Easter–Nov Sat–Sun 10.30am–12.30pm) in the community of Calozzo, where many of the various boat types used on the lakes are exhibited, including gondolas, fishing boats and punts.

GRAVEDONA

The historic centre of the upper part of Lake Como is ★ **Gravedona** (pop. 2,630), an independent commune during medieval times which later became famous for its goldsmiths. Right next to the lake is the **Palazzo Gallio**, built in 1583 and designed by Pellegrino Tibaldi.

Don't miss the church of ★ **Santa Maria del Tiglio** (open daily Jul–Sept 9am–6pm; at other times by arrangement with the tourist office) on the south side of the town: it is one of the most important Romanesque churches on Lake Como, and was originally an Early Christian baptistery (remains of mosaics and font). The striped facade is dominated by the tall, octagonal bell tower, and inside, a monumental 13th-century statue of Christ opens his arms in welcome. The neighbouring church of San Vicenzo dates from the 11th century, but was altered completely (apart from

Palazzo Gallio in Gravedona

the crypt) during the 17th and 18th centuries.

Gravedona is dominated by the church of **Santa Maria delle Grazie**, built in 1467 as part of an Augustinian monastery. It contains important frescoes by 15th- and 16th-century Lombard artists. A word of warning, though: it is hardly ever open.

Como to Lecco via Bellaggio

Como – Bellagio – Lecco (52km/32 miles)

The trips to Bellagio, the 'Pearl of the Lake', and to Lecco are both breathtaking, especially if you combine them with detours into the higher regions between the two arms of the lake – Monte San Primo, for instance (1,686m/5,530ft), or at least the Madonna del Ghisallo observation point (755m/2,480ft). The best views are to be had at Bellagio, the most famous resort on the lake, which has a perfect location and an unmistakeable charm of its own. Bellagio is best approached by steamer from Como. The roads along the lakeshore are very quiet, partly because of all their hairpin bends.

The villages along the steep shores are sleepy and harmonious, set against the blue backdrop of the lake, and there are far more old buildings than new ones. To really enjoy this route, allow two days and spend the night in Bellagio; those with less time could cover the ground in one day.

Star Attraction
● **Villa Carlotta**

Below: boating on a blue lake
Bottom: Torno

Map on page 52

PLINIANA

There are several villas between Como and **Torno**, among them the magnificent ★ **Pliniana** – which, by the way, has nothing to do with either Pliny the Elder or the Younger. The Pliniana was built in 1575 by Pellegrino Tibaldi, the architect who designed the villa for Como's governor Giovanni Anguissola. History books mention his involvement in the assassination in 1547 of the ruthless, sadistic Duke Pier Luigi Farnese (a son of Pope Paul III). The villa had several changes of owner after that, but also many illustrious guests, including Byron, Shelley, Stendhal, Napoleon, Liszt and Rossini – who wrote his opera *Tancredi* here in just six days. The villa is not open to the public.

The old part of Torno has many pretty corners. The church of **San Giovanni** is Romanesque in origin, with a 12th-century campanile, and was extended in the 15th century. Note the Early Christian tombstone in the nave.

Below: Nesso
Bottom: azaleas line the waterfront at Bellagio

NESSO

The views get better and better as you continue towards Bellagio. One very striking village is Careno, part of the municipality of **Nesso** (pop. 1,700), where the houses almost seem to be above rather than next to each other.

Above Careno is the entrance to the **Grotta Masera**, one of several caverns in this region. Up on the **Colma del Piano** (1,124m/3,687ft), 12km (7 miles) from Nesso, there is a magnificent view across the valleys and mountains surrounding Asso and Canzo.

BELLAGIO

The town of ★★★ **Bellagio** (pop. 3,000) lives up to its name. Its dramatic location at the point where Lake Como and Lake Lecco divide combines with the panorama, the villas and the gardens to produce an unforgettable sight. The Romans called it *Bilacus* ('between the lakes'). The promontory is best approached by boat, and it is clear why Flaubert wrote *on voudrait vivre ici et y mourir* ('one would like to live and die here') when he first caught sight of Bellagio.

The tiny *Borgo* (medieval village) lies on the western side of the narrow peninsula. Narrow flights of steps lead up from the lake promenade to the 11th-century parish church of **San Giacomo**, built by the *Maestri Comacini*. This three-aisled Romanesque structure with its 17th-century tower contains a very expressive *Entombment* attributed to Perugino (*circa* 1500).

VILLAS AND PARKS

The famous villas and ★★ parks of Bellagio have a varied history, such as the one surrounding the **Villa Giulia** on the eastern side of the peninsula, formerly the residence of Belgian king Leopold I and today in private hands. On the hill above the town is the ★ **Villa Serbelloni** (guided tours only of the gardens Apr–Oct Tues–Sun at 11am and 3.30pm), originally Renaissance but with neo-classical additions. One of the two villas owned by Pliny the Younger formerly stood on this site; later on it was converted into a Lombard fortress.

The entrance to the second large park in Bellagio, the one surrounding the ★ **Villa Melzi** (open late Mar–end Oct 9am–6pm) is located in the suburb of Loppia on the road to Como. The elegant

Best views
Alongside its villas and parks, Bellagio also has mountains, and the steep and rocky hinterland is ideal for hikes and excursions. Try a drive up to the **Madonna del Ghisallo** (755m/ 2,477ft) via Civenna, a delightful resort above the eastern arm of the Lario. The best place for a view of the triangle formed by Como, Lecco and Bellagio (Traigola Lariano) is the ★ **Monte San Primo** (1,686m/ 5,530ft), which offers a breathtaking panorama. The path to the summit can be reached by driving south from Bellagio and turning right in Guello.

The approach to Villa Melzi

Map on page 52

Map on page 52

Alessandro Manzoni

Manzoni's *The Betrothed*, generally esteemed as Italy's only major 19th-century novel, became a national institution. Such was Manzoni's fame that Verdi's *Requiem*, originally begun in memory of Rossini, was dedicated to him and was first performed in Milan in 1874, the year after his death. If you want to follow the trail of various buildings and scenes from the book, the tourist office produces a useful leaflet identifying the sites, many of which are in the village of **Olate**, lying east and above the town of Lecco.

Manzoni statue in Lecco

neoclassical villa was built in 1815 and is still privately owned, hence much of it is out of bounds to visitors. The park, dotted with statues, has a marvellous collection of exotic plants. Another romantic place is the **Buco dei Carpi**, a cavern down by the lake 5km (3 miles) out of Bellagio in the direction of Como, with attractive light effects reminiscent of the Blue Grotto on Capri.

LECCO

Continue onwards now via Malgrate to reach **Lecco** (pop. 46,200), with its smoking factory chimneys and traffic chaos. Very little remains of its former beauty these days, although its setting is dramatic. Nevertheless, Lecco is worth a visit, not least because it is the setting of *I promessi sposi (The Betrothed)* by Italy's greatest Romantic novelist, Alessandro Manzoni (1785–1873). Written in 1827, the book had immense patriotic appeal for Italians of the Risorgimento period, and is a portrayal of the struggle of two peasant lovers to marry, in the face of opposition from a vicious local landowner and the local priest.

Lecco has a few interesting sights. At the southwestern corner of the central square is the battlemented **Torre del Castello**, part of a former 15th-century Visconti fortress, and housing the **Museo del Risorgimento e della Resistenza**. The nearby **Ponte Azzone Visconti** also dates back to the days of the Visconti (1336–38).

In the suburb of Caleotti, **Villa Manzoni** (open Tues–Sun 9.30am–5pm) is where the author *(see above)* spent his youth. The 18th-century **Palazzo Belgioioso** (open Tues–Sun 9.30am– 2pm) contains the **Natural History Museum**.

SAN PIETRO AL MONTE

Lecco is indisputably ugly, but the scenery surrounding it is not. The lake, known as 'Lago di Lecco' reflecting the enduring rivalry between the towns of Como and Lecco, and the mountains are quite magnificent, and ideal for excursions. One to one-and-a-half hour's walk away from the village of **Civate** is the church of ★★ **San Pietro al Monte** (639m/2,100ft, open Sun 9am–3pm). Why a Benedictine monastery was founded here in this remote mountain region during the 8th century is not known, but the architecture blends in very harmoniously with the scenery.

Originally San Pietro was a hall church with an eastern apse; during the 11th century the entrance was switched to the eastern end to create direct access to the Oratorio San Benedetto, a centralised Romanesque structure situated further down. San Pietro's main claim to fame is its stucco and frescoes dating from the late 11th century, revealing the influence of Byzantine artists. The lunette fresco showing angels fighting a seven-headed dragon is very fine, as is the stucco work on the baldachin *(baldacchino)*.

THE GRIGNA

The ★ **Grigna** is the vast limestone massif next to Lecco, between the eastern shore of Lake Como and the Valsassina, and its highest points are the Grignone (2,409m/7,900ft) and the Grignetta (2,177m/7,140ft), both of them with a vast choice of hiking possibilities. The southern Grigna is particularly reminiscent of the Dolomites; an interesting three-hour route – for experienced climbers only – connects it with the Grignone.

Star Attraction
● San Pietro al Monte

Below: the garden of Palazzo Belgioioso in Lecco
Bottom: the Grigna massif

Map on page 52

The Fiumelatte

It's well worth stopping to admire the extremely short Fiumelatte River, or 'milk stream', just outside Varenna. From its source to the lake it covers a distance of just 250m (830ft), and this earned it a mention in Leonardo da Vinci's Codice Atlantico. Because of a geological phenomenon, its milky waters only flow between spring and autumn.

Steep steps in Varenna

The Eastern Shore

Lecco – Lierna – Varenna – Colico (41km/ 25 miles)

The stretch along the eastern shore of Lake Como can easily be covered in half an hour, thanks to the SS36 *autostrada*. Although the trip along its steep shores does give an idea of the sheer length of this post-glacial lake, to get to know the lake and its hinterland in a little depth, allow at least a day for this section.

Abbadia Lariana

After Lecco, the first town on the eastern shore of the Lago di Lecco – the name given to the eastern arm of Lake Como – is **Abbadia Lariana** (pop. 3,200). The name refers to a long-vanished Benedictine monastery; the oldest traces of settlement date back to pre-Roman times.

Most of the older buildings can be found in the upper part of the town, and there's a good view from the **Monte di Borbino** (486m/1,600ft), a 30-minute walk from the town centre. Abbadia Lariana's old silk factory, built in 1919, has now been turned into a small museum (Civico Museo del Setificio; open Sun 10am–noon and 2–6pm, except Aug: open some weekdays by arrangement, tel: 0341 731 241); a highlight is an enormous water-driven silk-spinning machine with 432 bobbins.

Mandello del Lario (pop. 9,500) has a number of worthwhile attractions: the parish church of San Lorenzo (9th, 12th and 17th-century), several old arcaded townhouses and also the richly decorated church of **Madonna del Fiume**, one of the best baroque buildings in the region. The smaller, 15th-century church of San Nicolò has some interesting late medieval features.

But Mandello del Lario's main claim to fame is its motor bikes – produced by the firm of Guzzi which was established here in 1921. The bikes have been successful for decades in races all over the world, and shining examples can be seen in the **Museo del Motociclo** on Via E. Parodi 57 (open Mon–Fri; free guided tours 3–4pm).

Further on, **Lierna** (pop. 1,500) is a very old area of settlement: Bronze Age artefacts and the foundations of a Roman villa have been discovered here. The small church in the suburb of Castello used to be part of a medieval castle.

VARENNA

At the widest part of the lake (4.5km/3 miles) lies ★ **Varenna** (pop. 841), with its picturesque centre of piled-up houses intersected by narrow alleys and dominated by the tower of the parish church of San Giorgio. This makes an excellent base for visiting the lake as it is the main ferry port. The basilica dates from around 1300, but underwent several alterations in the 17th and 18th centuries. There is a noteworthy *Baptism of Christ* (1553) altar painting here by Sigismondo de Magistris.

Just outside the town is the **Villa Monastero** (gardens open 25 Mar–1 Nov, daily 9am–7pm; closed when a conference is in progress), with its magnificent grounds; it is renowned for its citrus trees. The building was originally a convent, founded by the Cistercians in 1208 for nuns who had been evicted from Isola Comacina, and dissolved in 1567 because of the reputation for promiscuity gained by their successors. After several changes of ownership, the villa is now a conference centre.

Below: Varenna's waterfront
Bottom: Villa Monastero gardens

Map
on page
52

Bellano

Bellano (pop. 3,330) is home to the 14th-century parish church of SS Nazaro e Celso, whose black-and-white striped façade and rose window are worthy of note. However, the real tourist attraction here is the *orrido* of the torrent of Pioverna, a wildly romantic and very steep gorge (recommended only for those with a head for heights) just outside the town (the bridge is open June–Sept daily 10am–10.30pm; Oct–May Tues–Sat 10am–1pm and 3–6pm, Sun–Mon 10am–6pm).

Valsassina craftsman

ESINO LARIO

Don't miss a detour from Varenna to ★ **Esino Lario**. Situated at the top of a steep and winding road, this small town of many villas is sometimes known as the 'Pearl of the Grigna'. From the parish church there's a view westwards as far as Lake Lugano, and the peaks of the Grigna can be seen to the southeast.

The **Museo delle Grigne** contains some fascinating local Roman and Gallic finds, fossils, and minerals (open July–Aug daily 9am–noon and 4–7pm). Another excursion from Varenna goes via the 'Panoramica del Lario', and leads into the **Valsassina**, a magnificent southern Alpine valley.

PIONA ABBEY

Not far away from the relatively uninteresting industrial town of **Dervio** is the pretty village of ★ **Corenno Plinio**, which is said to derive its name from its early settlers who came from Corinth, and from Pliny the Elder who gave the site his highest praise. The church, ruined fortifications and quaint old houses are huddled together on a small rise next to the lake.

A bit further along, romantically perched on a peninsula, is ★ **Piona Abbey** (open daily 9am–12.30pm, 2–6pm). It was founded back in the 7th century, but the existing buildings are of far later origin: San Nicolò was consecrated in 1138, and its magnificent cloister dates from the 13th century. Today the abbey is occupied by Cistercians who, as well as attending to their religious duties, produce a liqueur called Gocce Imperial.

COLICO

The northernmost town on the eastern shore of Lake Como is **Colico** (pop. 6,500). The rough mountains round about lend it an almost Alpine appearance, and the ruins of the old fortress up on the **Montecchio** to the northeast of Colico blend in with the landscape. Originally built by the Spanish at the beginning of the 17th century, the fortress was destroyed in 1798 by the French.

6: Bergamo

Bergamo (pop. 114,200), known as *Bergomum* to the Romans, consists of the 'upper town' *(alta)*, which is the oldest part, and the more modern lower section *(bassa* or *piana)*. Originally a settlement of the Celtic tribe of the *Orobi*, it became a Roman town in 196BC. After its destruction by Attila it became the seat of a Lombard duchy, and in the 12th century the town became an independent commune.

From 1329 onwards the Visconti family ruled, but in 1428 it became Venetian property until 1797, when the French took control and included it in Napoleon's Cisalpine Republic. Bergamo owes much of its art and architecture to the legacy of Venetian rule. Between 1815 and 1859 the city was Austrian, then becoming part of the Kingdom of Italy. During Garibaldi's time, it was also known as the 'City of the Thousand' for its citizens' enthusiastic support for Il Risorgimento.

Bergamo was the home of the 16th-century Commedia dell'Arte, whose famous clowns include Harlequin, Pierrot, Pulcinella and Scaramouch. It is also home to the lusty, lively Bergamasque dance, which is still performed today.

Bergamo, a city steeped in history

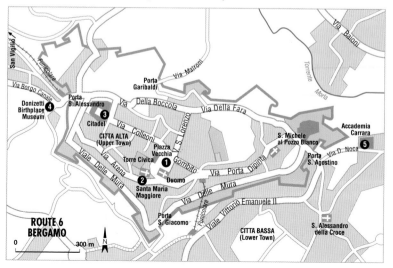

ROUTE 6 BERGAMO

Map on page 65

Accademia Carrara

In the lower town, Città Bassa, is Bergamo's cultural highlight, the ★★ Accademia Carrara ❺ (open daily Oct–Mar 9.30am–noon, 2.30–5.45pm, Apr–Sept 10am–1pm, 3–6.45pm). This art gallery, founded in the 18th century by Count Giacomo Carrara to house his collection of paintings, contains several superb works by artists such as Titian, Raphael, Botticelli, Bellini, Velázquez and Mantegna. Allow plenty of time for any visit here as it is one of the most important provincial galleries in the country.

Opposite the Carrara, the Galleria d'Arte Moderna e Contemporanea (open Tues–Sun Apr–Sept 10am–1pm and 3–6.45pm; Oct–Mar 9.30am–1pm and 2.30–5.45pm) hosts excellent touring exhibitions by contemporary sculptors and artists.

The rose window at Santa Maria Maggiore

CITY TOUR

The two parts of the city are linked by a funicular railway, rising from Viale Vittorio Emanuele II to the Città Alta in Piazza del Mercato delle Scarpe. The older, upper part is closed to traffic, and the best place to begin a stroll is the lovely medieval **Piazza Vecchia ❶**. The Venetian lions, on the **Contarini Fountain** in the middle, were erected in 1780 during the final years of Venetian rule by Mayor Contarini. It's worth climbing the steps of the **Torre Civica**, also known as Torre del Campanone (open Mar–Apr Tues–Fri 10am–12.30pm and 2–6pm; May–Sept daily 10am–8pm; Oct Sat–Sun 10am–6pm; Nov–Feb Sat–Sun 10.30am–4pm), for the view. Leave the Piazza Vecchia for the Piazza del Duomo, or Cathedral Square. Bergamo's Romanesque cathedral was rebuilt in 1483 and 1639; its white facade is almost completely hidden from view by the surrounding buildings.

SANTA MARIA MAGGIORE

Beside the Duomo is the 12th-century basilica of ★ **Santa Maria Maggiore ❷** (open daily 9am–noon and 3–6pm, till 4.30pm in winter), begun in 1137 and rebuilt during the 14th and 15th centuries. The red-and-white marble porch dates from the 13th century, and highlights inside the church include not only several magnificent 16th-century Flemish and Florentine tapestries, but also the tomb of Bergamo's most famous son, the operatic composer Gaetano Donizetti (1797–1848). Donizetti wrote 65 operas in his lifetime, and the most famous are probably *Lucia di Lammermoor* and *Don Pasquale*.

Lovers of architecture come to this church from all over the world to admire the ★★★ **Colleoni Chapel** (open Tues–Sun 9am–12.30pm and 2.30–6.30pm, till 4.30pm in winter), a Renaissance masterpiece built between 1470 and 1476 by Giovanni Antonio Amadeo, with ceiling frescoes by Tiepolo. Colleoni was a notorious *condottiere* (mercenary) who fought on several different sides during his successful military career, earning enough in the process to have himself suitably immortalised (his equestrian statue can be admired in front of the Scuola San Marco in Venice). The Piazza del Duomo also has a fine polygonal baptistery, built in 1340; it used to stand inside Santa Maria Maggiore.

Stroll westwards now as far as the Piazza Cittadella, where you will find the 14th-century **Citadel ❸**, which today houses a museum of geology and natural history, with several fascinating exhibits (Museo di Scienze Naturale; open daily except Mon: 9am–12.30pm and 2.30–7.30pm, 5.30pm in winter). The Torre dei Adalberto in this square was built in the 13th century, and is also known as the 'Tower of Hunger'.

Just behind the Citadel, beyond the the Porta Sant'Alessandro, is the **Donizetti Birthplace Museum ❹** at No 14, Borgo Canale (Casa Natale di Donizetti; open weekends 11am–6.30pm). The **Museo Donizettiano** (open Apr–Sept Tues–Sun 9.30am–1pm and 2–5.30pm; Oct–Mar am only) has his piano, bed (where he died), furniture and some portraits of the composer.

Bergamo's 'lower town' also has several attractions in addition to the Accademia *(see opposite)*, including the church of San Bartolomeo, with its large altarpiece by the Late Renaissance artist Lorenzo Lotto (1480–1556). Famous for his perceptive portraits and mystical paintings of religious subjects, he lived in Bergamo from 1513 onwards, and it was here that his style matured.

Star Attractions
● Accademia Carrara
● Colleoni Chapel

Below: Colleoni Chapel statues
Bottom: Donizetti remembered

Map below

Lakeside houses at Iseo

7: Lake Iseo

Lake Iseo, situated between Bergamo and Brescia, lies 186m (610ft) above sea level, is 25km (15 miles) long, has a maximum width of 5km (3 miles), a maximum depth of 250m (820ft), and a surface area of 62sq km (24sq miles). It contains the largest inhabited lake island in Europe.

LOVERE

This route goes clockwise around the lake, starting at the small town of **Sarnico**. The mountains along the quieter western shore descend steeply towards the lake, while the area of reeds across to the east is framed by rolling meadows. Local fishermen spend their days in search of lake tench – a speciality often served as *tinca al forno* (baked lake tench with polenta). Olive groves, vineyards and avenues of cypress line the road, which passes through a series of tunnels. The steep shore between Tavernola and Riva di Solto is unspoilt. Venice quarried the black marble for San Marco here, and until 1910 this region was only accessible by boat.

Soon the main town on Lake Iseo comes into view: **Lovere**, which has a well-restored Renaissance centre. This former textile town has made a successful transition to tourism, with a new marina on the lake. The church of **Santa Maria in Valvendra** is well worth a look for its baroque interior and Renaissance artwork. The **Galleria dell'Accademia Tadini** (open Apr–Oct Tues–Sat 3–7pm, Sun and hols 10am–noon and 3–6pm; Aug also Mon 3–7pm) has an astonishingly good collection of paintings, porcelain and Flemish tapestries.

ROUTE 7
LAKE ISEO
0   5km

Capo di Ponte,
Val Camonica
Lovere
Castro   Pisogne
Solto
Lago
di Endine
Riva
di Solto
Monte   Zone
Pendola   *Lago*   (Erosion
▲   Pillars)
1127
Monte   Marone
Isola   Sale
Tavernola   Siviano   Marasino
Berg.   Madonna
                   della Ceriola
Peschiera   Sulzano
Maraglio
d'Iseo
Sarnico   Iseo
            Provaglio
            d'Iseo
Adrò
F r a n c i a c o r t a
Torbiere   Bettole
Bergamo
Bornato   Gussago
A4
Brescia

MONTE ISOLA

The old road along the eastern shore winds pleasantly past several old villas as far as Pisogne, but then suddenly widens to accommodate heavy goods traffic. Don't rush at this point, otherwise you'll miss the 15th-century Augustinian church of ★ **Santa Maria della Neve** (open daily 7.30am–12.30pm and 3–6pm), which contains some fine fresco work by the 16th-century Renaissance artist Romanino and is sometimes known as the 'poor man's Sistine Chapel'.

The next stop is **Sulzano**, picturesquely situated beside a yachting harbour, and the starting-point for ferry trips across to ★★**Monte Isola** (Navigazione Lago d'Iseo steamers from Lovere and Sarnico also call at Monte Isola). This 'mountain-island', 600m (1,970ft) high and covered with chestnut forest and olive groves, is a haven of tranquillity. Allow a couple of hours to do the hike there and back from the village of Peschiera Maraglio to the 16th-century pilgrimage church of **Madonna della Ceriola** (300m/1,000ft). The ascent is steep but but well worth it for the views from the top.

Star Attraction
● Monte Isola

Island transport
Given the choice of ferry stops back to the mainland, you can opt to do just a short stretch of Iseo's waterside promenade (which is lined with fish restaurants). Perhaps enjoy a fish lunch in a rustic trattoria on the waterfront.

Below: ferry to Monte Isola
Bottom: life on the water

ISEO

A real highlight completes this brief tour of the lake: ★ **Iseo** itself, the most appealing town on the lake and good for restaurants, shopping and people-watching. The entrance to it via the 15th-century **Castello Oldofredi** is delightful. The various narrow alleys meet up at the arcaded **Piazza Garibaldi**, the town's medieval market-

Map on page 68

place, which is lined with inviting cafes and dominated by a mossy statue of Garibaldi.

CAPO DI PONTE

One very rewarding car excursion from the Lago d'Iseo is to **Capo di Ponte**, halfway up the Val Camonica to the northeast, famed for its **★★ prehistoric rock engravings**. Over 300,000 of these have been discovered, and they date from different periods – some even from Neolithic times (8,000 years ago). The engravings, many of which show hunting scenes and religious symbols, can be admired in Capo di Ponte's **National Rock Engravings Park** (Parco Nazionale della Incision Rupestri; open Tues–Sun Mar–mid-Oct 8.30am–7.30pm; mid-Oct–Feb closes 4.30pm), a UNESCO World Heritage Site since 1979.

> ### Erosion pillars
> For another fascinating sight, this time natural rather than man-made, drive inland from the eastern shore road at Marone and visit the attractive little village of Zone (678m/2,224ft). Just before the village of Cislano you'll see them: Zone's famous **★★ erosion pillars**, the finest examples in Europe. Created by the deposition of glacial debris, these fascinating natural columns vary in form, and their most unusual features are the boulders perched precariously on top, which make the whole scene even more bizarre.

Capo di Ponte

FRANCIACORTA

To the south of Lago d'Iseo, the region of **★★ Franciacorta** with its gentle morraine hills is a fascinating area to explore, bristling with palatial villas, parks and castles – and vineyards. In Bornato an old Roman fortress was enlarged in the 13th century into the **Castello di Bornato** (open Easter–Oct Sun 10am–noon and 2.30–6pm). Beautiful 16th- to 18th-century frescoes adorn the rooms, one of which Dante once slept in, while outside there are beautiful gardens and vineyards, which produce very good wine.

Just west of Lake Iseo lies the little Lago d'Endine and the small fascinating medieval town of **Monastero del Castello**, with its fine castle dating back to before AD1000.

From Iseo the most direct link with Lake Garda *(see opposite)* is via the road through Gardone Val Trompia, where the famous Beretta guns are manufactured, and on past the cliffs of Nozza, through Vestone to Lago d'Idro *(see page 93)*.

The **★ Strada del Vino Franciacorta** wine route covers 80km (50 miles), passing through the best estates to buy sparkling wine. For further details visit the excellent website www.stradadelfranciacorta.it.

8: Lake Garda

Map on page 72

Lake Garda, the largest lake in Italy, is 51km (31 miles) long, up to 17km (10 miles) wide and 65m (213ft) above sea level. Regarded by many as the most beautiful of the lakes, from its narrow northern end Lake Garda widens further south into a basin that is roughly oval in shape.

The rich flora on its southern and western shores include citrus fruits, laurels, cypresses, vines, oleanders, palm trees and olives. The lake was referred to as the *Lacus Benacus* by Virgil, Horace and Catullus, but its name changed in the 9th century when the city of Garda was elevated to a county by Charlemagne and acquired dominion over the lake. It is also known as *Benaco*.

Star Attractions
- **Capo di Ponte**
- **Franciacorta**

Below: carefree days by the lake
Bottom: restaurant in Riva

ENVIRONMENT

Three Italian regions border the lake: Trentino-Alto Adige, the Veneto and Lombardy. This has had a beneficial effect in that each province does its best not to be shown up by the others, and Lake Garda consequently has very well-surfaced roads and also a consistently successful environmental policy ever since the catastrophic pollution of the lake in 1992. The water quality is now acceptable, and a new environmental awareness has taken hold of the entire region.

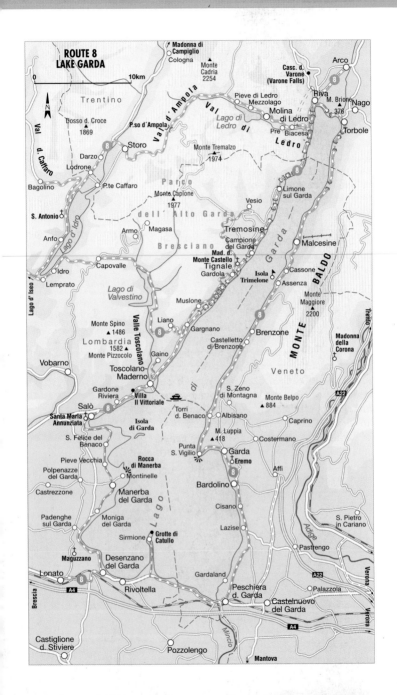

GEOLOGY

Lake Garda has an interesting geological history: the glacier that formed it broadened out as it reached the Plain of Lombardy and left a thick layer of moraine deposits. The lake then formed behind these – which explains why the southern part of Lake Garda is relatively shallow in comparison to the deeply gouged northern section (340m/1,115ft).

The lake is fed at its northern end by the River Sarca, and at the southern end the River Mincio flows out towards the Po. The entire basin contains 50 million cubic metres of water.

There are five islands in Lake Garda, all privately owned: the Isola del Garda (the largest one) in the west measures 9 hectares (22 acres), the Isola San Biagio in the southwest measures only 1 hectare (2½ acres) and the other three – Trimelone, Sogno and dell'Olivo – are so tiny that they are really only specks of rock.

ECONOMY

Tourism has had an enormous effect on the area around the lake over the past few decades. Lake Garda caters to over 5 million visitors each year (around seven percent of all tourists to Italy), so it's no surprise that the flatter eastern shore is full of hotels and campsites. The more elegant communities in the north and west continue to expand rapidly, and only strict building regulations have managed to halt the relentless construction of faceless apartment blocks and cheap hotels alongside medieval cathedrals.

This lake has for many years been closely associated with German and Austrian holidaymakers, who regard it as a Latin hothouse close to home. Nowadays equally popular with British tourists, Lake Garda is also the weekend haven for the landlocked residents of Brescia and Verona. Fortunately, despite the influx of outsiders, the region has retained its rural character and structure and, just a few miles inland, busy resorts surrender to peaceful vineyards, fields and orchards.

Map on page 72

Mediterranean Garda
For Goethe Lake Garda was (and still is) 'the land where the lemon trees flower'. Sheltered from the northern cold winds by the craggy Dolomites and open to the south, of all the Lakes this has the warmest and most Mediterranean of climates.

Below: tourists in Garda
Bottom: boats in Malcesine

The Eastern Shore

Riva – Malcesine – Torri del Benaco – Garda – Sirmione (75km/47miles)

The scenic stretch of road known as the Gardesana Orientale was completed in 1926, but today has sadly become one of the most-travelled routes in the region; mile-long queues are an everyday occurrence in peak season, but generous bypasses are gradually being built to cope with it all.

The route is varied in geographical terms, leading from Alpine mountains across rolling hills to the broad southern plain, and from the surfing paradises of Riva and Torbole, past the mighty Monte Baldo massif and the gentle Bardolino wine region, to reach the elegant thermal resort of Sirmione at the end of its narrow peninsula. Much of this route can also be covered by bus, and a day isn't really enough to fully appreciate all the contrasts. It's best to cover the eastern shore in stages, not forgetting the delights of 'real Italy' further inland.

Below and bottom: aspects of historic Riva

RIVA DEL GARDA

Tradition and elegance are the two most striking characteristics of ★★ **Riva** (pop. 15,000), situated at the northern end of Lake Garda, where the reflections of the steep foothills of the Alps shimmer in the turquoise water. Reminders of the

town's Roman origins are still visible in the old walls, whilst the old town's medieval tangle of little streets is flanked by the spectacular lakeside promenade. Riva has long been a favourite of writers and poets. Goethe called it a 'miracle of nature', and was followed here by Stendhal, Kafka and Thomas Mann.

As part of Habsburg Austria from 1813–1918, Riva del Garda was a popular resort for sun-starved northern Europeans, and was known as the 'southern pearl on the Austro-Hungarian Riviera'.

HISTORIC SIGHTS

The town has several interesting sights to offer, and the best place to begin any stroll is the ★ **Piazza III Novembre**, facing out towards the lake and the harbour, and dominated by the steep walls of the Monte Rochetta (1,540m/5,050ft). The other side of the square is taken up by buildings in the Venetian-Lombard style, with pleasantly cool arcades (14th-century) and the 34-m (111-ft) high Torre Apponale; this clock tower was formerly part of the town's fortifications. The 15th-century **Town Hall** (Palazzo Municipale) is connected by the Porta Bruciata to the 14th-century Palazzo Pretorio, and the coats of arms of the bishops of Trento and Venice can be seen on their facades.

Another worthwhile sight in Riva is the ★ **Chiesa dell'Inviolata**, a mighty 17th-century baroque building reached via the battlemented San Michele city gate, at the end of the Viale Roma. Relatively unadorned on the outside, this octagonal church has an incredibly ornate baroque interior that is well worth a visit.

The entrance to the ★ **Rocca**, a moated Scaligeri castle complete with drawbridge, is in Piazza Battisti. It was built in 1124 and has survived several alterations by the Viscontis, the bishops of Trentino and the Venetians. Today it houses the municipal library, a concert hall and also the **Museo Civico** (Civic Museum; open mid-June–mid-Sept daily 9.30am–6pm; mid-Mar–mid-June and mid-Sept–Oct Tues–Sun 9.30am–12.45pm and

Star Attraction
● Riva

Excursions from Riva
Just 5km (3 miles) north of Riva is the town of **Arco**, dominated by a 126-m (413-ft) high crag with the ruins of a medieval fortress, Castello di Arco, perched on top. The panoramic view is magnificent. In September each year, climbers congregate on the crag for the world climbing championships.

Just 4km (2 miles) outside Riva is the spectacular 87-m (285-ft) waterfall, **Cascata del Varone**, which can be admired from two grottoes. Warm, waterproof clothing is recommended. Another good excursion with a great view is to the top of Riva's local mountain, the **Monte Brione** (376m/1,230ft).

The Torre Apponale

Map on page 72

2.15–5.30pm; longer in summer when concerts are held in the castle), which has a collection of fascinating prehistoric finds from the pile dwellings at Lake Ledro *(see page 95)*, including some items dating from 4000BC.

Admission to the Rocca also includes entry to the **Torre Apponale** (piazza 3 Novembre; open Tues–Sun mid-June–mid-Sept 9.30am–6pm; mid Mar–mid Jun, mid-Sept–end Oct 9.30am–12.45pm and 2.15–5.30pm). From the top of the Tower there are spectacular views over the Lake.

Below: enjoying the lake at Torbole
Bottom: Malcesine's ancient charm

TORBOLE

Further down the lake, **Torbole** is the windsurfing capital of the region (it is on the World Cup circuit), and attracts fans of the sport from all over the world. For non-surfers it isn't the best of places, and can be rather noisy; wind and weather are of course the main subject of conversation here. The whole of the northern part of the Lake is one of Italy's top spots for windsurfing, with several schools that teach and hire out equipment.

The 18th-century parish church of Sant'Andrea contains a noteworthy *Martyrdom of St Matthew* by Giambettino Cignaroli above its altar. A short detour from Torbole leads up via the little village of Nago to the so-called ★ **Marmitte dei Giganti**, or 'Giants' Pots' – smooth holes in the rock created during the last Ice Age by swirling pebbles and meltwater.

MALCESINE

Now the so-called Riviera degli Olivi begins – the name refers to the stretch of lakeshore where high alpine scenery gently gives way to its Mediterranean equivalent, complete with olive trees – and the town of ★★ **Malcesine** (pop. 3,500) comes into view. This former fishing village now lives almost exclusively from tourism but, unlike many other communities, it has managed to preserve much of its ancient charm.

The mighty Scaligeri family from Verona, who once ruled this town like the Viscontis before them and the Venetians after them, left a magnificent monument behind: the ★★**Scaligeri Castle** (Rocca Scaligera; open June–Sept daily 9.30am–1pm and 4.30–7.30pm; Apr, May and Oct 9.30am–12.30pm and 2.30–6pm; closed Mon pm). Built originally in the 13th century, the castle's present form dates back to the 14th and 15th centuries.

Today the panorama from the top of the 33-m (108-ft) high keep can be enjoyed for the fabulous views of the surrounding walls and steep cliffs. It takes only a few minutes to reach the castle along the picturesque alleys of Malcesine, and the place is still remarkably intact, with an upper and a lower section and also three inner courtyards. The former powder room contains a small Goethe exhibition – in memory of the fact that his *Italian Journey* very nearly came to an end here *(see panel)*. Several of his sketches can also be admired.

The castle also contains the **Museo del Garda e del Baldo** (opening hours same as the castle), containing an exhibition on local wildlife.

HARBOUR HIGHLIGHTS

Down by the harbour, the **Palazzo dei Capitani del Lago** (open summer daily 9am–8pm), with its delightful palm garden, was once the seat of the Venetian governors. The entrance hall contains a fresco dated 1672 showing the castle of Malcesine

Star Attraction
● **Scaligeri Castle**

Goethe's lucky escape
Malcesine's fortress almost ended up costing Goethe his life. Delighted and fascinated by the sight of its mighty battlements, the famous German writer took out his sketch pad – and was immediately placed under arrest on suspicion of being an Austrian spy. Luckily one of the locals recognised his name, and he was released again. The event is now commemorated by a bust of the poet in the upper courtyard.

Malcesine from the water

Below: Casteletto courtyard
Bottom: the castle at
Torri del Benaco

crowned by the Lion of St Mark. The coat of arms of the governors and a fine wooden ceiling can both be admired in the council chamber on the first floor. The highlight of the 18th-century parish church of Santo Stefano is a 16th-century Pietà by the Veronese artist Girolamo dai Libri.

Excursions from Malcesine include the exciting *funivia* (cable car) trip up the 1,820-m (6,000-ft) **★★ Monte Baldo** (open Apr–Nov daily every 30 minutes 8am–6.45pm; journey time 10 minutes; tel: 045 740 0206). The panorama from 1,720m (5,643ft) is utterly breathtaking, the restaurants are good, and there's also a botanical garden 1,200m (3,937ft) up the mountain with around 600 different kinds of alpine flower.

The Gardesana continues southwards, lined with hotels, past several small villages such as **Cassone** (which has what many consider to be the shortest river in the world, the Aril, only 175 metres/574 feet long) and **Assenza**, as far as **Castelletto**, which is not on the lake but on the other side of the road, on the mountainside. It is a jumble of dark, medieval streets grouped around the Piazza dell'Olivo, with its delightful houses. South of Castelletto, visit the small 12th-century Romanesque church of **San Zeno**, which is something of an architectural rarity with its two aisles and three apses. It was built above Roman foundations, and the 15th-century frescoes depict biblical scenes.

TORRI DEL BENACO

The harbour town of **★ Torri del Benaco** (pop. 2,760) is dominated by another 14th-century Scaligeri castle, built above the foundations of a 10th-century fort. The attractively restored castle contains a **museum** (Museo Castello Scaligero; Apr, May and Oct daily 9.30am–12.30pm and 2.30–6pm; June–Sept 9.30am–1pm and 2.30–7.30pm) documenting everything from citrus fruit and olive cultivation to fishing and prehistoric rock drawings.

Just south of the castle is a very old *limonaia* (lemon garden). Other nearby sights include the baroque church of SS Pietro e Paolo, with its magnificent organ (1744), and the church of Santissima Trinità (at the upper end of the former Palazzo Gardesana) which contains several colourful frescoes dating from around 1400.

SAN ZENO DI MONTAGNA

From Albisano there is a highly worthwhile excursion up to one of the most beautiful views of Lake Garda. The poet Gabriele d'Annunzio referred to this place as the *Balcone del Garda*. Just 4km (2 miles) further on is the health resort of **San Zeno di Montagna**, with several cheap hotels – a good tip for anyone eager to flee the bustle of the shoreline. It's also the perfect base for hiking trips up Monte Baldo.

Enclosing the Bay of Garda to the north is one of the most delightful spots on the lake, the small promontory of ★★ **Punta San Vigilio**, complete with Sirens' rocks and a mermaid bay. The 16th-century Renaissance patrician, Agostino di Brenzone, had an elegant villa built here in the middle of a magnificent park; unfortunately it is still privately owned today and closed to public access. However, the house can still be viewed from the avenue of cypresses in the park. The chapel of San Vigilio can only be visited on 25 April each year.

Star Attractions
- Monte Baldo
- Monte Luppia
- Punta San Vigilio

Rock drawings
Several rock drawings dating from the Bronze Age were discovered in 1964 on ★★ **Monte Luppia** (418m/1,370ft), and over 250 rocks with more than 3,000 drawings have since been found. The rocks depicting swords and armed men are known as Pietre delle Griselle, and the ones with horsemen, Pietre dei Cavalieri. The rock drawings can be reached by taking the road to Albisano.

San Zeno di Montagna

Map on page 72

Wine and olives

To learn more about the delicious red Bardolino wine, visit the **Museo del Vino** (Via Costabello 9, Bardolino; open Mar–Oct daily 9am–1pm and 2–6pm). Also renowned for its olives, the area has a fascinating and informative **Olive Oil Museum** (Museo dell' Olio; Via Peschiera 54, Cisano di Bardolino, tel: 045 622 9047, open 9am–12.30pm and 3–7pm; closed Wed and Sun pm), which includes old lever presses and a reconstruction of an olive mill dating back to the 19th century, originally operated by water from Monte Baldo. There's also an excellent collection of earthenware containers and oil lamps, and the chance to sample (and buy) extra virgin olive oils.

Getting around Garda

GARDA

Continue southwards to the little town of ★★**Garda** (pop. 3,550), much appreciated for its medieval streets, trendy boutiques and elegant lake promenade. Garda takes its name from the Longobardic 'Warte', or fortress. As well as being one of the lake's most beautiful towns, it is possibly the oldest. The Rocca di Garda, a 294-m (964-ft) high rocky plateau, stands above the town like an oversized tower. Theodoric, king of the Ostrogoths, had a fortress built on top of it in the 5th century, but a few foundation walls are all that remains of it today. The tower played an important role in Italian history: here Adelaide, the widow of King Lotario, was held captive by his successor and murderer, Berenguer II, before she was rescued by Otto I of Germany in 951. Otto duly took Adelaide for his second wife, and they were crowned emperor and empress 11 years later, in 962.

Garda is full of noble villas and palazzi, most of which are privately owned. The finest one in town is the **Palazzo dei Capitani**, with its Gothic pointed-arch windows, in the Piazza Catullo on the lake promenade. The parish church of **Santa Maria Maggiore** in the Piazzale Roma outside the old town has a fine 15th-century cloister.

Garda has a backdrop of hills thick with olive groves, cypress trees and the famous Valpolicella vineyards. There is an excellent market on Friday, and most streets in the centre are traffic free.

MADONNA DELLA CORONA

A good excursion from Garda is **Eremo Monastery**, a.k.a. The Camaldolite Hermitage, founded in the 17th century. Recently, women have been allowed entry for the first time. To get there turn off at the Agip petrol station just outside Bardolino and travel as far as the village of Cortelline. There's a tiny road on the left near a statue of the Virgin which leads straight there.

The 16th-century pilgrimage church of ★**Madonna della Corona** is perched precariously 774m (2,540ft) above the Adige Valley. Get there via Costermano, which has one of the largest World War II military cemeteries in Italy, with over 22,000 graves. The church can be reached easily via Caprino Veronese, Spiazzi and then a short walk, or shuttle bus, for around 1km (½ mile). The first chapel was built here in 1530; heaving the construction materials up the mountain side must have been very arduous. Serious pilgrims take the steep 450 steps up from the Adige Valley.

Below: Bardolino facades
Bottom: inside San Severo

BARDOLINO

Next on this route is ★ **Bardolino** (pop. 6,190), at the centre of a wine region famed for its delicious light reds, as you can judge for yourself at one or more of the numerous tastings along the Strada del Vino, which makes its well-signposted way past 54 different vineyards. Highlights of the town of Bardolino include the 12th-century Romanesque church of ★ **San Severo** (open daily 9am–6pm), with its mighty campanile. The renditions of courtly battles, the Passion and the Apocalypse are amazingly lifelike. Beyond the high altar, the crypt has been excavated to reveal an earlier Lombard structure. The 9th-century chapel of **San Zeno** (Via San Zeno 13–15; open daily 9am–6pm) is tucked away in a courtyard: the building dates from the 9th century, and is one of the oldest surviving Carolingian structures in Italy.

Map on page 72

LAZISE

The romantic little town of ★ **Lazise** (pop. 6,150) has some well-preserved walls and a six-towered Scaligeri castle (12th-century, privately owned); under Venetian rule it was the most important trading post on the lake, and also the first independent commune. A 14th-century Venetian custom house and the 12th-century Romanesque church of **San Niccolò** both still stand as reminders of Lazise's heyday.

Inland from Lazise at Bussolengo is the **Parco Natura Viva** (open daily 9am–5pm, till 6pm in Aug; reduced hours in winter; closed Dec–Jan), a great family day out. Set up to protect endangered species, it contains a tropical bird park and a zoo.

PESCHIERA DEL GARDA

The former fishing village of **Peschiera del Garda** (pop. 8,800) has been strategically important since Roman times, and the 2.3-km (1½-mile) long bastion walls around its old centre were first built during Venetian times, and later strengthened by Napoleon and the Austrians. The best way to appreciate their sheer size is to take a boat trip along the moats.

Just north of Peschiera del Garda is Italy's largest and most popular theme park, **Gardaland** (open April–mid June, last two weeks of Sept 10am–

Above: niche statue in the Lazise town gate
Below: on the waterfront

6pm; mid-June–mid-Sept 9am–midnight; Oct Sat–Sun 9am–6pm; www.gardaland.it). Pirates, dinosaurs, roller coasters, waterparks and a dolphinarium make this is a great family day out.

Star Attraction
● **Sirmione and its castle**

SIRMIONE

The town of ★★★**Sirmione** (pop. 7,000) is like something straight out of a fairytale. It lies at the very end of a flat, 4-km (2½-mile) long peninsula which widens at the end to form three rocky crags rising from the brilliant blue of the water.

The bright colours of the flowers, and the green of olives, laurels and cypresses, combine with the red of the rooftops and the soft light to create a unique Mediterranean atmosphere, all of it set against the incomparable beauty of the high Alps in the distance.

ROCCA SCALIGERA

The old centre can either be reached either along the peninsula road, with its hotels and supermarkets, or more romantically by boat from Desenzano. The first sight that strikes visitors here is the magical ★★**Scaligeri moated castle** (or 'Rocca Scaligera'; open Apr–Oct Tues–Sun 8.30am–6.30pm; Nov–Mar 8.30am–4.30pm), one of the best-preserved fortresses in Italy, bristling with battlements and turrets. It was built by Mastino I della Scala in 1250, above the foundations of the former Roman harbour. A massive 30-m (98-ft) high keep towers above the castle walls, and there's a stunning ★ panorama from the top that takes in the peninsula and the whole southern half of Lake Garda. The **castle museum** (open Apr–Sept daily 9am–12.30pm and 2–6pm; Oct–Mar Tues–Sun 9am–1pm) contains several finds from antiquity and also a 15th-century Venetian galley.

The old town, with its jumble of alleyways and enchanting houses, is reached through just one gate, and the lake can be glimpsed now and then between the buildings. The town gets less busy towards the thermal baths, and there are several

Literary Sirmione
The poet Catullus voluptuously enjoyed life and called Sirmione 'the pearl of all islands and peninsulars'. The sexually explicit nature of many of his poems made him notorious to generations more prudish than his own. However, the heady atmosphere around Sirmione has always been an inspiration for many writers, from Romantics such as Dante, Byron and Goethe to modernists such as Ezra Pound and James Joyce, few of whom have suffered from any prudishness.

Sirmione's Scaligeri castle

Maps on pages 72 & 85

Below: San Pietro in Mavino
Middle: Grotte di Catullo
Bottom: Custoza

gardens on the way down to the Grotte di Catullo. High up on the nearby hill is the small Romanesque church of ★ **San Pietro in Mavino** (open daily 9am–sunset), built by Lombard monks in the 8th century; the frescoes date from the 12th to the 16th centuries, and there is a particularly impressive *Last Judgement*.

GROTTE DI CATULLO

On the edge of the peninsula is the Spiaggia Lido della Bionde (open daily May–Oct from 8am), a 'beach' for swimming and sunbathing. At the very end of the peninsula are the remains of an enormous Roman villa (230m/755ft long, 105m/345ft wide), known as the ★★ **Grotte di Catullo** (open Mar–mid-Oct Tues–Sat 8.30am–7pm, Sun 9am–6pm; late Oct–Feb Tues–Sun 8.30am–4.30pm). Famous for his magnificent love poems and satiric verse, not to mention his scurrilousness and wit, Gaius Valerius Catullus (87–54BC), who was born in nearby Verona, surely knew of this complex of buildings, which was probably an imperial guest house or even an imperial palace, complete with its own thermal baths.

A large swimming pool in the vast complex was fed by the Boiola springs on the lake shore via lead piping. The sulphurous springs were rediscovered in the 16th century, but only re-used 300 years later. Since that time, visitors to Sirmione have been able to enjoy bathing in hot spring water. The small museum (same opening times as the Grotte, except June–Sept Sat 2.15–11.45pm) has pieces from the ruins of the villa in addition to prehistoric and medieval artefacts from the peninsula and Lake Garda.

BATTLE SITES

There are reminders of the wars against the Austrians all over the region, in villages such as Custoza and Solferino. Surrounded by meadows and vineyards, ★ **Custoza** lies on a small rise. Former battle sites such as these are known in Italy as Zona Sacra, or 'holy zones'. The monument, with its enormous obelisk, commemorates the death of thousands of soldiers.

It was in July 1848 that Count Radetzky's Austrian troops inflicted a crushing defeat on Italy's freedom-fighters. An **ossuary** (open daily except Tues; Nov–Feb 9am–noon and 2–4pm, Mar and Oct 9am–noon and 2.30–5pm; Apr– Sept 9am–noon and 3.15–7pm) to house the remains of the fallen was built here 30 years later; it contains the bones of 3,200 soldiers of both nations.

PONTE VISCONTEO

The next stop on this route is **Borghetto di Valeggio sul Mincio**, a sleepy village in the shade of Valeggio's Scaligeri castle which was chosen 600 years ago as the site of a demonstration of power. In 1393 Giangaleazzo Visconti decided to build a gigantic dam to deprive the cities of Mantua and Verona of water. The dimensions are amazing: the ★★ **Ponte Visconteo**, as the dam is called, is 600m (1,970ft) long, 26m (85ft) wide and 10m (33ft) high, and it took just eight months to build. It's worth taking a stroll across the dam, with its gates and towers, to get a close-up impression of this astonishing medieval achievement. In 1438, not even the Venetians dared attack the Ponte Visconteo to help besieged Brescia fight the Visconti. Instead, Venice was clever and bold enough to transport 6 galleys, 2 galleons and 26 barques – pulled by 2,000 oxen – across the Nago Pass, and then re-float them near Torbole. This amazing feat is celebrated in an exhibition at the castle in Malcesine *(see page 76)*.

Star Attractions
- ● **Grotte di Catullo**
- ● **Ponte Visconteo**

Madonna del Frassino
Before following the River Mincio southwards, take a detour to tiny Laghetto di Frassino, and one of the most delightful pilgrimage churches in the region, ★ **Madonna del Frassino**, built in the early 16th century. It is said that the Virgin Mary appeared in an ash tree *(frassino)* here in 1510 and saved a vintner from a poisonous snake. A side-chapel, with a miracle-working Madonna sculpture standing on the original ash tree's branches, is filled with candles.

The ossuary at Custoza

Map on page 85

One destination worth considering for an excursion is the ★★**Parco Giardino Sigurtà** (open Mar–Nov Thur, Sat, Sun and public holidays 9am–6pm), an English-style park in Veneto covering 50 hectares (125 acres). It has small lakes, viewing terraces, a hermitage church and yet another ruined Scaligeri castle.

SOLFERINO

Henry Dunant
On the night of 24 June 1859, Henry Dunant of Geneva stopped at Castiglione, 8km (5 miles) west of Solferino, in the midst of the Liberation's bloodiest battle. He and volunteers from the village helped some 6,000 wounded from both sides. Dunant returned to Geneva fired with enthusiasm for establishing a work force of impartial volunteers to help the wounded, and finally in 1863 the International Committee of the Red Cross was founded. He received the Nobel Peace Prize for his efforts in 1901, and promptly donated the prize money to his organisation. The great humanist did not live to see the horrors of World War I; he died in 1910 in Appenzell.

It was the battle of ★**Solferino** that prompted Henry Dunant to found the Red Cross (Croce Rossa; *see adjacent box*). The Chiesa San Pietro in Vincoli contains the remains of around 7,000 soldiers who fell here. By way of contrast, the **Museo Storico** (open Mar–Oct Tues–Sun 9am–noon and 2–6.30pm, winter till 5.30pm) glorifies war, with plenty of weapons, uniforms, and the history of Italy from 1796 to 1870.

The ★**Piazza Castello**, one of the finest squares in the province of Mantua, was formerly occupied by an 11th-century castle. All that remains of the original building today is one watchtower with an oriental-style pointed cupola. The marble Red Cross Memorial, erected here in 1959, can be reached along an avenue of cypresses; the **Museo Internazionale della Croce Rossa** (Red Cross museum) is at Via Garibaldi, 50 in nearby Castiglione delle Stiviere (open Wed–Mon 10am–5pm).

The last famous battle site in this region is **San Martino della Battaglia**, which shared Solferino's fate in 1859. A 74-m (243-ft) high tower stands in memory of the horrors of war. Inside, wall frescoes document the history of the Italian freedom fighters from 1848 to 1870.

Remnants of battle at San Martino della Battaglia

The Western Shore

Desenzano del Garda – Salò – Gardone Riviera – Limone – Gargnano (70km/44 miles)

From Salò to Riva alone, a total of 70 tunnels had to be blown out of the rock to build the road along Lake Garda's western shore. Car drivers may be rather confused at all the light and shade, but passengers will glimpse a whole series of superb Mediterranean-style vistas. Even in heavy traffic the route can easily be covered in an hour, not including detours. Visiting only a few of the sights can easily take up a day, however.

DESENZANO DEL GARDA

The town of ★ **Desenzano del Garda** (pop. 25,000) at the southwestern end of Lake Garda is the largest and also the liveliest community on the lake. A harbour since Roman times, the town is still a busy trading centre. Its enormous market is held every Tuesday on the Cesare Battisti lake promenade; the selection of wares is vast.

Near the main square, at the end of the Via Crocefisso, are the ruins of ★ **Villa Romana**, northern Italy's finest later Imperial villa. It was begun in the 1st century BC but mainly dates from the 3rd century AD (open June–Oct Tues–Sat 8.30am–7.30pm, Sun and public holidays 9am–6pm; Nov–May Tues–Sun 8.30am–5pm). The 240sq-m (2,600sq-ft) of mosaic floor reveal the magnificence of Roman lifestyles during Late Antiquity, and represent the most extensive example of mosaic floor in Northern Italy. It's also well worth visiting the 16th-century cathedral of **Santa Maria Maddalena** (open daily 9am–noon and 4–6pm) on

Star Attraction
● **Parco Giardino Sigurtà**

*Below: mosaics at
the Villa Romana
Bottom: Desenzano drifters*

the Piazza del Duomo; it contains an impressive early work by Tiepolo, *The Last Supper*, as well as murals by the Venetian artist Andrea Celesti.

Bog dwellings
A museum at Desenzano del Garda (Museo Archeologico Rambotti; cloister Santa Maria de Senioribus, Via Anelli 7; open Tues and Fri–Sun 3–7pm) shows new evidence of the Bronze Age dwellings discovered in the peat bogs south of the town.

LONATO

Lonato (pop. 11,400) is a typical Lombard town 10km (6 miles) to the west of Desenzano. It was here in 1796 that Napoleon inflicted a crushing defeat on the Austrians. There is a fine view across the Plain of Lombardy from the ruined fortress.

On the way up there, you pass the ★ **Fondazione Ugo da Como** (Via Rocca 2, open daily 10am–noon and 2.30–6.30pm; www.fondazioneugodacomo.it), a neo-Gothic folly and shrine to the Middle Ages created by the austere aesthete, Ugo da Como (1869–1941). The beautiful residence with its stunning interior overlooks the Rocca, a Venetian fortress, and is of more interest than Lonato itself.

Just 5km (3 miles) north of Lonato is the ★ **Abbazia di Maguzzano**, a formerly Benedictine abbey built in the 9th century, destroyed in 922 by the Huns and then plundered yet again by the Visconti in the 14th century. It received its present appearance in the 15th century, and the church and cloister are magnificent. Dissolved by Napoleon in 1797, the abbey fell into decay before being purchased by the Cistercian Order in 1904.

Stop for coffee

WINE REGION

North of Desenzano is the rolling Valtenesi, a fertile region famous for its pale red Chiaretto wines, olives and white truffles. Ruined fortresses on the hilltops testify to a violent past. **Moniga del Garda**, hidden behind its battlemented walls, is one of the most attractive communities. **Manerba del Garda** is a tourist centre, and there's a good view from the ruined **Rocca di Manerba** (218m/715ft) near Montinelle. Don't miss the 15th-century pilgrimage church of ★ **Santa Maria del Carmine**, 13km (7 miles) north of Pieve Vecchia, in the middle of a vineyard region; it contains a fine *Annunciation* by a local 15th-century artist, as well as a delightful wooden Madonna.

Map on page 72

SALO

Continue now to the delightful town of ★★ **Salò** (pop. 10,200). It suffered a minor earthquake in 2004 but has since been restored, and its extended waterside promenade is now the longest (and arguably the best) on Lake Garda. Start your stroll at the cathedral of **Santa Maria Annunziata** (open daily 9am–noon and 3.30–6.30pm), the most important Late Gothic structure in the region. Note the 11-m (36-ft) high Gothic-Venetian dome. Highlights inside include a Late Gothic crucifix dating from 1449, and an interesting *St Antony of Padua* by Romanino (1486–1562), in which the artist breaks with convention by portraying his patron most unflatteringly as a fat, unpleasant-looking man at St Antony's feet. Also by Romanino is a *Madonna and Child with Saints Bonaventura and Sebastian*. The Palazzo Fantoni houses the Biblioteca dell'Ateneo di Salò and the important **Museo del Nastro Azzurro** (Via Fantoni 49; open summer Tues, Thur, Sat and Sun 10am–noon and 3.30–5.30pm; winter Thur, Sat and Sun 10am–noon and 3–5pm). This museum charts military history from the late 18th century to 1945.

GARDONE RIVIERA

The town of ★ **Gardone Riviera** (pop. 2,400) became the most fashionable resort on Lake

Star Attraction
● Salò

Below: Santa Maria Annunziata
Bottom: Manerba from the Rocca

Map on page 72

Mussolini's last stand
Salò is also famous historically as the place where Mussolini's Nazi-supported puppet government continued to rule a reluctant Italy from 1943 onwards. The order to proclaim the Italian Social Republic came from Hitler, but its sphere of influence dwindled steadily as the German troops were forced back. When the German front in Northern Italy finally crumbled, Mussolini was forced to flee to Switzerland with his mistress Clara Petacci. They were caught by partisans in Dongo, on Lake Como, and executed in Mezzegra *(see page 56)*.

Giardino Botanico bloom

Garda in the late 19th century, due to the Grand Hotel Gardone Riviera, built by the German architect Ludwig Wimmer in 1880. Today, its mild climate, lovely promenade and pretty harbour have ensured its enduring popularity.

The upper part of town contains **Il Vittoriale degli Italiani** (open Apr–Sept gardens daily 8.30am–8pm, house tours Tues–Sun 9.30am–7pm, museum tours Thur–Tues 9.30am–7pm; Oct–Mar gardens daily 9am–5pm, house tours Tues–Sun 9am–1pm and 2–5pm, museum tours Thurs–Tues 9am–1pm and 2–5pm; www.vittoriale.it), a bombastic monument commissioned just before the war by Fascist Italy's most celebrated poet, Gabriele d'Annunzio. The Vittoriale is a gloomy monument to its flamboyant owner's megalomania, its rooms a mixture of priceless antiques and glorified kitsch. The complex includes a theatre, a columned hall containing his mausoleum, a domed structure to house the private plane he used to distribute leaflets above Vienna in 1918, a museum full of memorabilia, and also the bow section of a ship. It is part of the battleship *Puglia*, filled with cement and uncannily realistic. The eclectic collection contains many peculiar objects, including a mirror aimed at the visiting Mussolini, inscribed 'Remember that you are made of glass and I of steel'.

Only a few steps away from the Vittoriale is the wonderfully peaceful **Giardino Botanico Fondazione Andre Heller** (Via Roma 2, tel: 336 410877, open Mar–Oct daily 9am–7pm; www.hellergarden.com). Its waterfalls, ponds and bridges combined with some 8,000 exotic plants and Alpine flora make it an oasis of tranquillity. Dotted around the gardens are some bizarre installations created by Austrian artist Andre Heller.

TOSCOLANO-MADERNO

The main attraction of Toscolano-Maderno is the 12th-century parish church of ★★ **Sant'Andrea**, on the lake promenade in Maderno. Fragments of an Early Christian temple, and also the remains of an earlier Lombard structure, can be recognised from the facade, apse and westwork. The entrance portal has some fine sculpture work. Toscolano, the other half of this twin-town, grew rich during medieval times by making metal components for Venetian galleys, and then even richer from its paper and printing industry, which started here in the 15th century and is still flourishing today.

Star Attraction
● Sant'Andrea

GARGNANO

The picturesque resort of ★ **Gargnano** (pop. 3,000) has so far been left relatively unscathed by tourism, but is famous for its lush Mediterranean vegetation, as well as its windsurfing and sailing *(see also Festivals page 109)*. From 1943 to 1945 the neo-classical Palazzo Feltrinelli housed the offices of the Fascist 'Republic of Salò'; today, Milan University holds its language courses there during the summer. Mussolini lived in the **Villa Feltrinelli**, just a short walk away, which is now the grandest hotel on Lake Garda. Another of Gargnano's highlights is the Romanesque-Gothic **cloister of San Francesco** (open late July–late Aug daily 10am–1pm and 3–8pm, otherwise 9am–6pm), where citrus fruits adorn the stone columns in place of the usual demons and gargoyles.

Below: Sant'Andrea interior
Bottom: Villa Feltrinelli

MADONNA DI MONTE CASTELLO

For adventurous motorists, there's an exhilarating excursion from Gargnano to the 13th-century

Map
on page
72

*Below: Madonna di
Monte Castello
Bottom: a head for heights
is essential*

(later turned baroque) pilgrimage church of ★★**Madonna di Monte Castello**. Situated 700m (2,290ft) above sea level, it lies at the end of a road full of bends, and there's a brief gradient of 26 percent just before you arrive. The church was built above the ruins of a Scaligeri fortress, and the ★★ view is absolutely incredible.

TREMOSINE

From here, continue on to ★**Tremosine**, the collective name for several villages in the Campione valley. Many coins and also the 'Stone of Voltino', with Latin and Etruscan inscriptions (now in the Roman Museum in Brescia), were found here, testifying to settlement of this region in ancient times, when it was used as a place of refuge. Today, it is still off the beaten track: its hairpin bends continue to deter tourist buses.

A warning to all motorists without a head for heights: the roads often pass steep drops and require not only good nerves but also good driving abilities. Hooting before each hairpin is obligatory.

Of all the small villages with incredibly good views around here, **Pieve** deserves special mention. Those prone to vertigo should avoid dining in Pieve's 'Miralago and Benaco' restaurant, despite the excellent food: the restaurant terrace juts out above a vertical drop of 350m (1,150ft).

LIMONE SUL GARDA

Back down at the lake is the busy little town of **Limone sul Garda**. Formerly the lemon garden of Lake Garda, the local economy today revolves around tourism. **Limonaia del Castel** (via Orti, open daily 10am–5pm) is a tribute to the imposing stone-and-wood *limonaie* (lemon houses) that once covered this part of Lake Garda. Both lemons and larger fruit called citrons have flourished around the lake since the 13th century.

The 17th-century parish church of **San Benedetto** (open daily 9am–6pm) in the centre is worth a visit for Andrea Celesti's *Three Magi* on the right of the altar. By the way, don't leave Limone sul Garda without sampling its delicious carp dishes, flavoured – of course – with lemon.

Some Smaller Lakes

Gargnano – Lago di Valvestino – Lago d'Idro – Lago di Ledro (80km/50 miles)

As a change from the crowds on the busy shores of Lake Garda, a trip to some of Lombardy's smaller lakes is very rewarding. Generally speaking, mass tourism has passed them by. This route leads from Gargnano on Lake Garda to the Lago di Valvestino, on to the Lago d'Idro, which only has communities along its western bank, up to the tiny Lago di Ledro, with its prehistoric pile dwellings, and then back to Lake Garda. Allow three hours for the trip.

LAKES VALVESTINO AND IDRO

From Gargnano, it is a short way to **Lake Valvestino**, a reservoir set between the Val Toscolano and the valley of the Valvestino. The green, fjord-like waters of the lake contrast most impressively with the dam, and the whole scene is framed against magnificent mountain scenery. There are great views to be had from the top of Monte Caplone, reached from Magasa.

The next lake on the route is the ★ **Lago d'Idro**, known to the Romans as the *Lacus Eridius*. The steep mountain cliffs that surround this lake seem

Limone waterfront

Map on page 72

Smaller Lakes
Lake Tovel is a beautiful little lake in one of the most unspoilt landscapes of Trentino. Until recently it was famous for the blood red colour of its waters in summer, due to the presence of algae. There are very pleasant walks in the surrounding woods.

Lake Toblino is perhaps the most romantic lake in the area, a place where many famous poets and artists have found inspiration. Mirrored in the lake is the Castel Toblino, perched on a rocky outcrop. This is famous for the tragic love affair between Carlo Emanuele Madruzzo and Claudia Particella that resulted in drowning. Today the castle is partly converted into a restaurant that serves local specialities.

Lake Molveno is picturesquely set in the lee of the Brenta Dolomites. Famous mountaineers such as Francis Ford Tuckett and Edward Theodore Compton have stayed here.

to rise straight out of the deep-blue water in places, and some sections of shore are impassable. Although The Lago d'Idro is the highest of the large lakes in Lombardy (at an altitude of 386m/1,200 ft), its water temperature is similar to that of Lake Garda, some 300m (985 ft) lower down, reaching around 25°C (77°F) during the summer. It is particularly renowned for its trout.

Lake Idro is popular with campers, and there are several sites dotted around the main resort village of **Idro**. The nearby village of **Anfo** is rather more pleasant than Idro itself, and attracts a great many sailing enthusiasts. The small chapel of **Sant'Antonio** nearby contains 15th- and 16th-century frescoes, but is usually closed.

Ponte Caffaro, 2km (1 mile) before the northern tip of the lake, is where the Counts of Lodrone did battle first with the Milanese and then the Venetians, and Italy's former border with the then Austrian-ruled Trentino was located here until 1918.

Just outside the village of Anfo, up on the Rocca d'Anfo, is a castle originally built by the Venetians during the 15th century. In 1866 Garibaldi made it his headquarters, and during World War I it was used for military purposes again in the fight against the Austrians. It is closed to the public.

BAGOLINO

There's a good detour 16km (10 miles) westwards at this point to ★★ **Bagolino**, which was very wealthy in medieval times because of the iron ore mined in this valley. The detour there begins with several superb views across the lake. Bagolino has a fine 18th-century church and several elegant town houses, reflecting the past prosperity of the settlement. A strong cheese, called Bagoss, is made in the mountains around the town.

Continue along the western shore of Lake Idro now and at Ca Rossa, turn right on to the road leading to Lake Ledro. This route takes you through the Val d'Ampola, past several waterfalls and high mountains (Monte Cadria, 2,254m/7,395ft) as it winds its way steadily uphill. From Tiarno the road then descends to Lake Ledro.

LAKE LEDRO

★**Lake Ledro** is only 3km (2 miles) long, 1km (½ mile) wide and up to 48m (150ft) deep, but is surrounded by some stunning mountain scenery, and is also important historically as the site of several lake dwellings. The lake was formed when the valley was blocked by the moraine of the Garda glacier. Lake Ledro's waters are full of fish and are a splendid iridescent green in colour.

For centuries the fishermen of Lake Ledro were irritated by the wooden stakes that kept getting caught in their nets, but no-one realised what the wood was actually doing there. When the water level was lowered in 1929 during a hydro-electric project, the remains of over 15,000 piles were discovered.

It turned out that people had lived here in 1700BC in a prehistoric village on the lake, and the piles had supported the entire structure. Pottery, axes, amber jewellery and other finds from the lake and its surrounds are on display in the ★★**Lake Dwelling Museum** (Museo delle Palafitte, Pieve di Ledro; open Mar–June & Sept–Nov Tues–Sun 9am–1pm and 2–5pm; July–Aug daily 10am–6pm) in the village of Molina di Ledro.

From Lake Ledro it's not far to the Cascata del Ponale waterfall and back to Lake Garda.

Star Attractions
- **Bagolino**
- **Lake Dwelling Museum**

Below: Fishing at Lake Idro
Bottom: Lake Ledro

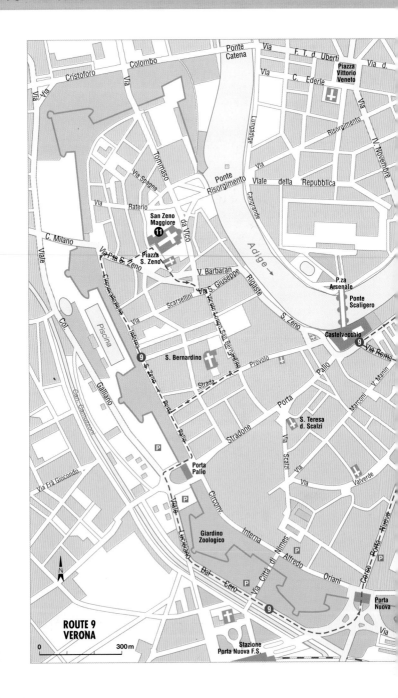

**ROUTE 9
VERONA**

0   300 m

Via Nino Bixio

San Giorgio in Braida 8

S. Stefano

Castel S. Pietro

Mille

Via Santo

Via Prato

Via Matteotti

Ponte Garibaldi

Archbishop's Palace

Piazza Vescovado

Biblioteca Capitulare 6 5

Ponte Pietra

Museo Archeologico 7

Teatro Romano

S. Giovanni in Valle

Panvinio

P.za Duomo

Cathedral of Santa Maria Matricolare

9 Via Duomo

V. Ponte Pietra

Via Redentore S. Chiara

Lungadige

Basilica Sant'Anastasia 4

Via Sottoriva

V. Pigna

9 9

Via Scala Giardino

Garibaldi

C. S. Anastasia

Santa Maria in Organo

Giardino Giusti

Lungadige Ponte

S. Eufemia

Emilei

Via

Arche degli Scaligeri 3

S.M. Antica

P.za Indipendenza

Teodorico

Acqua

Via Giusti

10 Palazzo Giusti

Ponte d. Vittoria

Lungadige

Porta Borsari

Corso Pta Borsari

i

Piazza dei Signori

Piazza delle Erbe

Ponte Nuovo

Morta

Carducci

Via Muro Padri

Corso Cavour

Via Oberdan

Cattulo

Via Mazzini

Stella

2 Casa di Giulietta

Lungadige Rubele

9

Interrato dell'

Via

Porta Borsari

V. Mario

Anfiteatro

Via

Leoni

Porta Leoni

Lungadige Sammicheli

Arena 1

S. Nicolò

Liston

Leoncino

S. Fermo Maggiore

Ponte Navi

XX Settembre

Via

S. Paolo

Museo Lapidario Maffeiano

Piazza Brà

i

Municipio

Str. S. Fermo

Palazzo Pompei

Pertoni di Bra

Pal. d. Gran Guardia

V. d. Alpini

Str. Mattei

Adige

Via Filippini

Via Vittoria

Università

P

Via Bentegodi

Via Montanari

Via Don Bertoni

Via Pallone

Ponte Aleardi

P

Gattarossa

Pta

Via F. Torbido

Cimitero

Via Battisti

Via

Via Pontiere

9

12 Tomba di Giulietta

Lungadige

Monumentale

SS. Trinità

Via Zappatore

Via dei

Via Lanciere

Via Fante

Giardini Pubblici Raggio di Sole

Ponte S. Francesco

Lungadige

Franco Faccio

Map
on pages
96–97

9: Verona

Situated on a sharp bend in the River Adige, Verona is an ancient city with Roman remains that are second only to those of Rome itself – the city is often called 'Piccola Roma'. It was also a renowned centre of painting in medieval times, but is perhaps most famous of all as the backdrop to Shakespeare's *Romeo and Juliet*.

HISTORY

Below: Piazza Brà facade
Bottom: wet night at the opera

Verona is located at a point of great strategic significance, at the junction of main roads between Italy and Europe. In 89BC it became a Roman colony, and this marked the start of its 'Golden Age', which lasted as long as Roman rule itself: from the 1st century BC to the 5th century AD. During this time *Colonia Augusta* received its municipal charter, became the capital of Cisalpine Gaul and developed into an important trade and administration centre.

After the Romans left, it was occupied by the Visigoths, then the Byzantines, and then the Lombards. After a Carolingian interlude the Lombards returned once more.

Medieval times were beset by feuds between rival families. In 1277 the della Scalas gained the upper hand and ruled for over a century. It was

during this period that the Scaligeri castles, still such a striking feature of the region, were built. Peace returned when Verona voluntarily submitted to Venetian domination in 1405, and it continued until the arrival of the French in 1796.

After Napoleon's defeat in 1814, Verona found itself in Austrian hands and the fortifications were strengthened. 1866 brought Italian unification, and although the Austrians still clung on until 1914, their final hopes were dashed by the outbreak of World War I.

THE CENTRE

This tour begins at the **Piazza Brà**. It's the longest of the three piazzas and also contains the most sights, so set aside half a day. Entrance fees are charged for most sights. *Chiese Vive*, an association of several churches, offers a combined ticket, which is cheaper than buying separate tickets.

THE ARENA

Verona's famous ★★ **Arena ❶** (open Sept–June Tues–Sun 9am–6pm; July–Aug Tues–Sun 8am–3.30pm; Mon 1.45–7.30pm), completed in AD30, is the third largest in the world after the Coliseum in Rome and Santa Maria Capua Vetere near Naples. Originally it was 152m (498ft) long, 123m (403ft) wide and could accommodate 30,000 spectators. Today, two thousand years and several earthquakes later, it is still 138m (452ft) long and 109m (357ft) wide, and still has room for 20,000 people.

Even those with very little time for sightseeing should try to fit in a visit to ★ **Castelvecchio**, the largest fortress/palace dating from the time of the Scaligeri, the medieval rulers of Verona, which now houses the ★ **Museo di Castelvecchio** (open Tues–Sun 9am–7pm), Verona's most famous art museum. It contains works by masters of the Veronese and Venetian schools from the 13th to the 18th century (paintings by Pisanello, Veronese, Mantegna, Tintoretto, Tiepolo, and others), all hung magnificently.

Star Attraction
● **The Arena**

Gladiators
The Arena was used for a very different entertainment in Roman times. Gladiators fought to the death, and bloody combats were arranged between wild beasts and men and, later, for the martyrdom of Christians. Today it is the site of the world famous open- air Opera Festival, but as you look down from the 44 tiers of the arena, you can still see the maze of underground passages and cells where man and animal paced, until finally being winched into the auditorium to do the ultimate battle.

Below: Arena arches
Bottom: museum exhibit

Map
on pages
96–97

> **The English connection**
> Although Romeo and Juliet are fictional characters, Shakespeare's feuding families were based on the real life characters of the Montecchi (Montagues) and Cappelli (Capulets).
>
> Many generations later, the 19th-century English writer John Ruskin fell in love with the city, enthusing over the 'serenity of effortless grace' of the Renaissance buildings and the foaming Alpine river 'from whose shore the rocks rise in a great crescent, dark with cypress and misty with olive.'

In the courtyard of Juliet's House

JULIET'S HOUSE

At the end of the Via Mazzini, Verona's most elegant shopping street, stands the ★★ **Casa di Giulietta ❷** (open Tues–Sun 8am–7pm, longer in summer) with the most famous balcony in the world (Via Capello 23), where Shakespeare's Juliet is supposed to have lived.

Today's picturesque ★★ **Piazza delle Erbe** used to be the old Roman forum, and is named after the ancient city's herb market. The architecture here is wonderfully harmonious. The Gothic Colonna del Mercato is a 14th-century obelisk built under the Visconti rule; the Capitello, a late 15th-century marble baldachin in the centre of the square, was used as an official meeting-place and also as a pillory in its time. The statue on the middle fountain dates back to Roman times, and the piazza is ringed by various official and very elegant palazzi. There is a Venetian lion on top of the marble column at the northern end of the square.

PIAZZA DEL SIGNORI

A high arch, the Arco della Costa, marks the entrance to the ★ **Piazza dei Signori**. The Venetian governor used to reside in the Renaissance Palazzo del Tribunale (1530). Today the Palazzo del Governo, where Dante lived in 1303, is the seat of the provincial government. The Dante café, next door to the magnificent Loggia del Consiglio, is a good place to soak up the atmosphere.

For the best view of the Piazza dei Signori, climb the distinctive 12th-century tower, **Torre dei Lamberti**, next to the Palazzo del Comune (open Mon 1.30–7.30pm, Tues–Sun 9.30am–7.30pm).

The next small square, the Piazzaletto delle Arche, contains the Gothic graves of the Scaligeri, the ★ **Arche degli Scaligeri ❸**, concealed behind wrought-iron grilles (admission included with the Torre dei Lamberti). There are even some set into the facade of the 12th-century Romanesque church of Santa Maria Antica. Romeo's house, also 12th-century, is nearby, at Via Arche Scaligeri 2–4.

THE CATHEDRAL

The ★ **Basilica Sant'Anastasia** ❹ (open Mon–Sat 9am–6pm, Sun 1–6pm), at the end of the arcaded Via Sottoriva, was completed in the 15th century by the Dominican Order. It contains Pisanello's celebrated *St George Fresco* to the right of the main choir. Not far away stands the ★ **Cathedral of Santa Maria Matricolare** ❺ (open Mon–Sat 10am–5.30pm, Sun 1.30–5.30pm), originally a Romanesque structure built above a 5th-century Early Christian church. Don't miss the superbly colourful ★ *Assumption of the Virgin* by Titian in the first side-chapel of the north aisle. Just next door to the cathedral is the ★★ **Biblioteca Capitolare** ❻ (open Mon–Sat 9.30am–12.30pm), thought to be the oldest surviving library in the world, with manuscripts dating from the 4th and 5th centuries and some wonderful miniatures.

ALONG THE ADIGE

This tour starts on the other side of the **Ponte Pietra** and leads to the best viewpoints in the city. Walking the route takes at least 3 hours, doing it by car takes around 1 hour (parking spaces are available).

On the other side of the bridge on the left is Santo Stefano, founded in the 5th–6th century and one of the oldest churches in Verona, and almost straight

Star Attractions
- **Casa di Giulietta**
- **Piazza delle Erbe**
- **Biblioteca Capitolare**

Below: Basilica Sant' Anastasia detail
Bottom: Ponte Pietra

Map
on pages
96–97

ahead are the ruins of the **Teatro Romano** ❼ (open Mon 1.30–7.30pm; Tues–Sun 8.30am–7.30pm). Built in the 1st century BC, the Roman theatre was used as a quarry in medieval times, then forgotten about until the 19th century. Shakespeare plays are often performed here during the summer.

SAN GIORGIO IN BRAIDA

A lift from the Teatro Romano goes up to the **archaeological museum** (open Tues–Sun 8.30am–6.30pm, Mon 1.30–7.30pm) in the monastery of San Girolamo. It is worth visiting for the finds and for the magnificent view across the city.

Below: Palazzo Giusti
Bottom: getting around town

The 16th-century church of ★★ **San Giorgio in Braida** ❽, with its cupola by Sanmicheli, has been described as the finest Renaissance building in Verona. Highlights inside include a *Baptism of Christ* by Tintoretto and a *Martyrdom of St George* altar painting by Veronese. During his Italian Journey, Goethe noted that San Giorgio was 'a gallery full of good paintings'.

The next two stops on the tour are further up the Adige: firstly the church of ★ **Santa Maria in Organo** ❾, formerly Benedictine, which gained its earliest written mention in 866, and received its Renaissance splendour from Sanmicheli at the end of the 15th century; and secondly, the ★ **Giardino Giusti** ❿ (open daily summer 9am–8pm; winter 9am–sunset), the gardens of a beautifully situated 16th-century palazzo, high up above the city in terraced grounds, with a stunning panoramic view over a wooded hill and ravine and terraces.

FURTHER SIGHTS

The starting-point for this tour is the Porta Palio, a city gate dating from the 16th century. Travel round the Circonvallazione to the Piazza San Zeno and the basilica of ★★★ **San Zeno Maggiore** ⓫ (open Mon–Sat 8.30am–6pm, Sun 1–6pm). This is one of the most magnificent Romanesque churches in Northern Italy. After a previous building on the site was destroyed in the 9th century, the new basilica was completed in 1138. Of the incredible number of frescoes inside the basilica, the 15th-century ★ *Madonna and Child with Saints* triptych by Andrea Mantegna deserves special mention; the music-making angels at the Virgin Mary's feet have marvellously touching expressions. The facade of the basilica is also quite magnificent. The ★★ bronze door, with its 48 reliefs, and the ★★ stone reliefs by Master Nicolò (12th-century) on either side of the portal are fascinating. Inside, the left-hand side-aisle leads off to a very fine ★ cloister.

THE TOMB OF JULIET

The last sight on this route is the ★ **Tomba di Giulietta** ⑫ in the cloisters of San Francesco al Corso (open Tues–Sun 8.30am–7.30pm, Mon 1.30–7.30pm). Legend has it that Romeo and Juliet were secretly married in the former Franciscan monastery on the Via del Pontiere. In the middle of an atmospheric courtyard stands an old fountain into which visitors throw coins; in the crypt is an empty stone sarcophagus labelled the 'Tomb of Juliet', which receives lovers' written petitions from all over the world. The small museum here (**Museo degli Affreschi**; opening hours same as above), with an extensive collection of frescoes, altar paintings and Roman amphorae, is worth a visit.

Star Attraction
● San Zeno Maggiore

Veronese patron
The basilica was consecrated to Verona's first bishop and patron St Zeno, who died in 380AD. The marble sculpture of this Black African saint, dating from the 14th century, is found at the end of the north aisle; it is venerated by the Veronese as a symbol of their town.

Below: bronze door detail, San Zeno Maggiore
Bottom: Juliet's empty tomb

Art and Architecture

Architecture in the Northern Italian Lakes region began with early lake dwellings such as those in Lake Ledro. It was around the same time that the rock drawings appeared on Monte Luppia and at Capo di Ponte. Later, the Romans left several magnificent monuments such as the ruined villa at Desenzano, the thermal baths in Sirmione and the Arena in Verona. Verona's remains are only surpassed by Rome itself. Most buildings are made of stone, and an early example of just how gifted the local masons were, after the fall of the Roman Empire, is the 5th-century baptistery in Riva San Vitale, the oldest sacred building in Switzerland.

ROMANESQUE

Dark but clearly proportioned churches, richly decorated portals and porches, and square bell towers on the facades are characteristic of the Lombard Romanesque style in the 11th and 12th centuries. Around Garda, the style culminated in the basilica of San Zeno Maggiore in Verona (perhaps the finest Romanesque structure in northern Italy), San Severo in Bardolino, and San Pietro in Mavino in Sirmione.

GOTHIC

Originally French, the Gothic style first established itself in Lombardy in the mid-13th century. While the Italian Gothic adopts the French pointed arch, it generally dispenses with exterior flying buttresses, maintaining the solid walls typical of the Romanesque. The Lombard builders also ignored the upwards-striving style of the Gothic, preferring classical horizontal lines and broad interior spaces. The gradual transition to Gothic is seen in Santa Maria Matricolare, in Verona.

Around Lakes Maggiore and Garda, the Gothic seemed to have been less influential. However, the cathedral in Salò (1453–1502), and the church of San Francesco in Gargnano (13th-century), are both fine examples of the High Gothic style.

> **Maestri Comacini**
> In the area around Lakes Maggiore and Como during the 12th and 13th centuries, it was the Lombard craftsmen known collectively as the *Maestri Comacini* who determined the local style. These expert stonemasons, who came from Como and are known to have been working at least as long ago as the 7th century, also began to influence styles throughout Europe, establishing a legacy that was to continue right up to the Renaissance and Baroque eras. The great baroque architect Francesco Borromini, who left such a mark on Rome, was himself a Como master craftsman.

Opposite: Verona Arena
Below: San Zeno Maggiore

RENAISSANCE

In around 1400 Florentine builders began to replace the Gothic style by adopting classical motifs and features. Rounded arches, classical columns and a great emphasis on the horizontal, achieved for example by cornices, are typical components of the Renaissance style. It gradually made its way across Northern Italy to Lombardy, and Leonardo da Vinci and Bramante were the two artists who helped Renaissance art to flourish here; their students continued the tradition in many buildings and works of art. In the Maggiore region, the most important works dating from this period are the facade and choir of Como cathedral, and also Castiglione Olona near Varese, the 'mini-Florence' commissioned by Cardinal Branda Castiglione.

In Verona the Renaissance flourished, with architects such as Michele Sanmicheli and Fra Giocondo producing some incomparable work, including the portal of Salò cathedral and the Loggia del Consiglio (1485–92) in Verona. Many small rural churches built in the Romanesque and Gothic styles were given Renaissance alterations during this period. The facade of the cathedral of San Lorenzo in Lugano is a good example.

> **👁 Baroque and neo-classical architecture**
> Two historical highlights of the Baroque era are the parish churches of Limone and Riva on Lake Garda. In Varese, the Palazzo Estense is another fine example of the style. The neoclassical movement is best exemplified by the Palazzo Oliginati in Como and the Villa dell'Olmo. During the 19th century, Milan assumed a leading role in architectural development; the Risorgimento and Italian unification meant that very little was built outside the city. Nevertheless, Varese did receive an attractive art nouveau hotel at the turn of the century, the 'Campo dei Fiori'.

20TH-CENTURY ARCHITECTURE

During the Mussolini era the pomposity of Fascism was accompanied by very sober and oppressive architecture, exemplified in Como by the Novocomum (1927–29), the Casa del Fascio (1932–36), the Sant'Elia Kindergarten (1936–7) and the Casa Ascheri (1936). The centre of Locarno was redesigned by Mario Cereghini in 1937.

In the Ticino, some modern architecture uses local construction materials, such as granite, very successfully. Mario Botta is one of the more famous exponents of the 'Ticino School'; his Cappella Santa Maria degli Angeli, situated 1,567m (5,140ft) above Lake Lugano, is stunning. Botta's residential houses in the Ticino are designed rather like caves; he refers to them himself as *caverne magiche*. Their strict design is based on mathematical forms such as cubes, prisms and cylinders.

Como Cathedral

Literature and music

One of the most important Italian poets of the 18th century was the Lombard Giuseppe Parini (1729–99), whose elegant satires were emulated by Carlo Porta (1775–1821) in his dialect poetry. From the 19th century, Alessandro Manzoni (1785–1873) from Milan occupies a leading position, both because of his historical novel *The Betrothed*, set on Lake Como and considered the most notable novel in Italian literature, and also his religious writings. The actor and playwright Dario Fo was born near Lake Maggiore. Famous works include *Accidental Death of an Anarchist* (1970) and *A Woman Alone and Other Plays* (1991).

Below: Donizetti
Bottom: a packed Arena di Verona

The introduction of certain musical elements into church worship by Archbishop Ambrose (339–397) of Milan was of immense importance. In more recent times the development of opera has been closely linked with Lombardy, and with Milan's Teatro alla Scala in particular. The Bergamo-born Gaetano Donizetti (1797–1848) and Giuseppe Verdi (1813–1901), who chose Milan as his home, Amilcare Ponchielli (1834–86) and Umberto Giordano (1867–1948) are just some of the famous names to be associated with operatic life in Lombardy. Just as famous are the star conductor of the Scala, Arturo Toscanini (1867–1957), and cellist Enrico Mainardi (1897–1976).

Festivals

31 January: traditional boat procession; San Giulio, Lake Orta.

February: Carnival in Arco; processions and masks scare away winter, evil spirits, etc. Other carnival sites are Bagolino, Como and Bergamo-San Giovanni Bianco, home of the harlequin, where they make a bonfire of the masks.

March: Festa di mezza quaresime takes place in Limone; a Lentern festival where a great deal of fish (especially deep-fried sardines) and white wine are consumed.

April: San Giulio near Stresa holds its **flower festival**. The **exhibition of camellias** at Verbania, Lake Maggiore, launches the tourist season. **Good Friday processions** take place in Castelletto di Brenzone and Biazza, where the Passion is re-enacted in torchlit olive groves; the **concert and theatre season** opens in Sirmione and Malcesine; the **Pasqua Musical Arcense** concert festival begins in Arco.

May: San Filippo Neri in Torri del Benaco; a festival in honour of the local patron saint. A boat and thousands of floating candles are set alight.

June: an **Early Music Festival** is held in San Giulio, Lake Orta. The **Festa del Pesciolino** occurs on the last Sunday in June in Limone, with fish and white wine served up for free in the Piazza Garibaldi. Isola Comacina, the weekend after the

The Opera Festival in Verona

This, the major cultural event of the year in the Garda region, takes place from late-June to early-September (www.arena.it), with bus trips organised to the performances from every major town on Lake Garda. Remember, however, that tickets for star performers are sold out the moment box offices open.

Performance of Nabucco at Verona's Arena

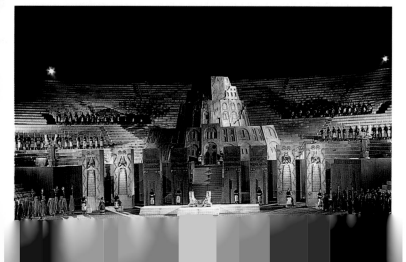

feast of St John the Baptist (24 June), celebrates the **commemoration of the destruction of the island's city in 1169**, with fireworks symbolising the battle and a religious procession. Between June and October, Como holds a **medieval music festival**. From the end of June to early July Ascona stages the **European Jazz Festival**.

July: **Estiva Jazz**; a jazz festival is held in the Piazza della Riforma in Lugano. A classical **Musical Festival** also occurs in Lugano. **Drodesera Festival** in Dro, near Riva del Garda, featuring modern dance and theatre as part of the Trentino Festival. **Estate Musicale** in Salò; a series of classical concerts.

August: International Film Festival in Locarno, held on the Piazza Grande. The best international film is awarded the *Golden Leopard*. **Festa di Sant'Ercolano**, the festival of the town's patron saint on 11 and 12 August, with firework displays in Toscolano-Maderna; on 15 August the **Palio delle Contrade** is held, a traditional boat race between the towns on Lake Garda. **Settimane Musicale** in Stresa, with ensembles from all over the world performing, take place over five weeks from late August to the end of September. Concerts are given both in the town and in the magical setting of the lake shores.

September: Verbania Corso Florita takes place on the first weekend of the month; consisting of flowers, concerts, folklore and fireworks by Lake Maggiore. **Sagra dei Osei**, a whistling and singing contest held 8–9 September in Cisano near Bardolino; the competitors must dress as birds and compete with the real thing. Over the first half of the month, the **Palio Baradello** traditional boat races take place on Lake Como. The second week of the month sees the **Gargnano Centomiglia Regatta** on Lake Garda, the most prestigious regatta held on Italian lakes.

October: Festa dell'Uva wine festivals held on the first weekend of the month in all wine regions around the lakes, e.g. Bardolino. This is the time to buy vast quantities of very good wine cheaply. The **Settimane Musicali di Ascona**, a classical music festival, is held in mid-October.

Publicity for Lugano's vibrant cultural life

FOOD AND DRINK

Lombard cuisine is as varied as the landscape. The western side of Lake Maggiore is in Piedmont, with its truffles, *grissini* and Barolo wine. There are regional specialities here too, of course: a favourite local dish at Lake Orta is *tapulon* (minced donkey meat braised in red wine). Perhaps a little more appealing to a British palate are *trotella alla Savoia* (trout on mushrooms) and the Lake Iseo speciality *tinca al forno* (baked tench with polenta).

TRADITIONAL FAVOURITES

Lombardy is the home of some well known traditional favourites which have influenced the cuisine in neighbouring Ticino: *ossobuco* (shin of veal braised in a tomato and wine sauce), *risotto alla milanese*, or the *costoletta alla milanese*. This last was first mentioned in a Lombard cookbook dated 1134 as *lombolos cum panitio*, discovered in the 19th century by the Austrian field-marshal Radetsky and introduced to the Austrian capital as the *Wiener Schnitzel*.

A speciality of the Varesotto is *faraona alla Valcuvia*, partridge baked Valcuvia-style, traditionally in a soft clay container. Around Verona the *risotto* comes into its own. For a taste of home cooking, *cazzoeula* (pork stew) is deliciously filling.

FISH AND CHEESE

Fish is of course an integral part of the cuisine around the Italian lakes. *Agonia alla Comasca* (baked and marinated shad), *anguilla del pescatore* (stewed eel), *lavarelli al vino bianco* (lake fish in white wine), *pesce in gelatina* (fish in aspic) and *suppa di pesce alla tremezzina* (fish soup) are just a few of the numerous fish specialities. A typical Lake Como delicacy is *curadura* (salted and dried

shad), a former 'poor man's meal' which has now become something of a gourmet speciality. The delicate Lake Garda trout known as *carpione* should be sampled too.

For dessert, one of the best ways to wind up a meal is with a *panettone* (yeast cake) from Milan. Another option is to order a rich *tiramisù* or *i brutti e i buoni* (biscuits served with a glass of Amaretto liqueur).

Italy produces excellent cheeses, and local *gorgonzola* or *bel paese* are always a good bet. Lombard cheeses include *grana* (the Lombard version of Parmesan), *mascarpone* and *stracchino*. The *formaggini* (fresh cheeses flavoured with oil and hot paprika) from Ticino are particularly good; *robiola* comes from the Valsassina and soft *gaprini* comes from the Brianza (which also does very good salami).

WINE

Lombardy's reds are particularly good. In Ticino the top wine is a ruby-red Merlot. Bardolino, Valpolicella and Soave (of varying quality) are all produced around Verona. Bianco di Custoza is an elegant Soave from the eastern shore of Lake Garda. The reds of Trentino are excellent, especially Tesoldego and Schiava.

A popular grape south of Lake Garda is Trebbiano, which makes an excellent dry white. Lugana has a particularly good, fresh dry white. A light, fizzy rosé is produced in the Valetnesi region north of Desenzano, and two more fine wines are the robust white Tocai del Garda and the versatile Recioto from Val Policella. Choosing a *vino della casa* (house wine) is a good bet in a restaurant: it is usually dry, light and 'honest'. One good one is Nostrano, from Ticino.

Restaurant selection

The restaurants recommended below are listed according to four categories: €€€€ = more than €60 per person, €€€ = €40–60, €€ = €25–40, and € = €25 or less. Major credit cards accepted unless otherwise indicated.

Arona
Trattoria Campagna, Via Vergante 12, tel: 0322 57294. 4km (3 miles) northwest of Arona in Campagna; very good Piedmontese food. Closed Mon evening (except July and Aug), Tues, 15–30 June and 10–25 Nov. €€

Ascona
Osteria Nostrana, Piazza Motta, tel: 091 791 5158. On the central square, overlooking Lake Maggiore. Pizza and pasta are served in a traditional, cheerful atmosphere. €–€€
Ristorante Aphrodite Hostaria Giardino, Albergo Giardino (Relais et Châteaux), Via Segnale 10, tel: 091 791 0101. Beautiful restaurant, adorned with statues, serving Piedmontese specialities. Good wine list includes crisp, dry whites from the Ticino. Must book. €€€–€€€€

Bardolino
Aurora, Piazza S. Severo 1, opposite S. Severo, tel: 045 721 0038. Veronese cuisine, fresh lake fish and meat in friendly restaurant. Closed Mon. €€
Al Commercio, Via Solferino 1, tel: 045 721 1183. Good, simple trattoria. €
Il Giardino delle Esperidi, Via G. Mameli 1, tel: 045 621 0477. This stylish restaurant combines creativity with seasonal, local specialities. There is also a menu for gourmands and an excellent wine list. Lovely outdoor terrace in summer. Closed Wed lunch and Tues; booking advised. €€–€€€

Bellagio
Ristorante Mistral, Grand Hotel Villa Serbelloni, Via Roma 1, tel: 031 956435. A Michelin-starred restaurant on the shores of Lake Como. Ettore Bocchia creates innovative 'molecular' cuisine. Closed lunch June–Sept, and Dec–Feb. Fixed menu on Friday (€40 excl drinks), otherwise €€€€

Como
Gatto Nero, Via Monte Santo 69, Rovenna (3km/2 miles inland from Cernobbio), tel: 031 512042. Gloriously situated in the hills with beautiful views. Specialities are fish, meat and an excellent cheeseboard. Closed Tues lunch and Mon; must book for evening. €€€
Ristorante Raimondi dell'Hotel Villa Flori, Via Cenobbio 12, tel: 031 338233. Elegant restaurant in attractive villa with great views; classic Italian cuisine. Closed Mon and Sat lunch Mar–Oct. €€€€
Sant'Anna 1907, Via Turati 3, tel: 031 505266. Young, dynamic team offering innovative cuisine in an elegant restaurant. Closed Sat lunch and Sun; must book for evening. €€€

Desenzano del Garda
Cavallino, Via Murachette 29 (corner of Via Gherla), tel: 030 912 0217. Specialises in seasonal and regional dishes, with excellent lake fish and seafood. Closed Sun eve, Mon and 5–23 Nov; booking advised. €€€€

Garda
Locanda di San Vigilio, Punta San Vigilio, tel: 045 725 6688. Intimate little inn with tables facing the lake. Fine food, especially the pasta and buffet. Closed Tues and Nov–Feb. €€€–€€€€
Al Pontesel, Via Monte Baldo 105, tel: 045 725 5419. Pizza, pasta and traditional Italian fare. Closed Wed. €
Stafolet, Via Poiano 9, tel: 045 725 5427. Good regional cooking in a romantic tavern; good pizza and grilled dishes. Closed Wed and Nov. €

Gardone Riviera
Villa Fiordaliso, Corso Zanardelli 150, tel: 0365 20158. Excellent, Michelin-starred food in lovely lakeside surroundings. Closed Mon and Tues lunch, and Nov–mid-Feb; must book. €€€€

Gargnano

La Tortuga, Via XXIV Maggio 5, tel: 0365 71251. Expensive but one of the best in the region, with one Michelin star, located near the port, where fish is a speciality. Closed Tues, lunch July–Aug, and mid-Nov–end Feb; reservations essential. €€€–€€€€

Iseo

Gualtiero Marchesi, Via Vittorio Emanuele 11, Erbusco, tel: 030 776 0562. This Michelin-starred temple to gastronomy is set on a wine estate in Franciacorta. Everything here is done to perfection as you would expect from Italy's celebrated chef, Gualtiero Marchesi. Closed Sun eve, Mon, and 3 Jan–10 Feb; must book. €€€€

Il Volto, Via Mirolte 33, tel: 030 981462. A small *osteria* with one Michelin star, serving excellent, inventive food. Closed Wed and Thur lunch, and first two weeks in July. €€€–€€€€

Laveno

Concordia, Piazza Marchetti 7, tel: 0332 667380. Good value and popular with locals. Closed Mon, Jan–mid-Feb and Nov. €–€€

Il Porticciolo, Via Fortino 40, tel: 0332 667380. Splendid views from this elegant restaurant; lakeside dining in summer. Closed Tues (except lunch July and Aug) and Wed, and end Jan–early Feb; must book. €€€

Lazise

Botticelli, Via Rocca 13, tel: 045 758 1194. Atmospheric, rustic restaurant where the speciality is fish from both sea and lake. Closed Mon (except July–Sept) and Jan. €€–€€€

Il Porticciolo, Lungolago Marconi 22, tel: 045 758 0254. Good regional cuisine in picturesque setting. Closed Tues, and late Dec–early Feb. €€

Lecco

Ristorante al Porticciolo, Via Valsecchi 5/7, tel: 0341 498103. Wonderful fresh fish is the speciality in this Michelin-starred restaurant. Closed Mon, Tues, lunch (except holidays), first two weeks in Jan, last two weeks in Aug; booking essential. €€€

Trattoria Vecchia Pescarenico, Via Pescatori 8, tel: 0341 368330. Simple, welcoming trattoria specialising in seafood. Lake fish can be ordered in advance. Closed Mon, lunch, 10 days in Jan, and last two weeks of Aug; booking advised. €€–€€€

Limone sul Garda

Gemma, Piazza Garibaldi 12, tel: 0365 954014. Family-run for almost 50 years, this restaurant is on the picturesque lakeside square. Specialities are grilled salt- and freshwater fish platters as well as home-made pasta. Very popular, with a faithful clientele. Closed Dec–Feb. €€

Locarno

Casa del Popolo, Piazza Corporazione, tel: 091 751 1208. Popular eatery, frequented by the local politicians. Wide choice of pizzas as well as pasta and good-value traditional Italian dishes. No credit cards. €

Centenario, Lungolago 17, Muralto, tel: 091 743 8222. Some of the best Italian and French food in the Swiss Lakes. Closed Sun and Mon; reservations essential. €€€–€€€€

Cittadella, Via Cittadella 18, tel: 091 751 5885. A popular trattoria serving good value pizzas, pasta and simple fish dishes. Upstairs the formal restaurant has very good fish. Closed Mon. €–€€

Svizzero, Piazza Grande. Best of the many pizzerias and diners on the square, with fresh pasta and wood-fired pizza. No booking. €

Trattoria da Luigi, Via Dogana Vecchia 1, tel: 091 751 9746. Ticino cuisine in pleasant surroundings. €€

Lugano

Motto del Gallo, Taverne, 13km (8 miles) from Lugano on the road to Bellinzona, tel: 091 945 2871. Atmospheric restaurant specialising in good, home-made pasta, fresh fish and meat dishes. Closed Sun; reservations recommended. €€€

Grotto dei Pescatori, Caprino (boat for Gandria, get off at Caprino/Grotta dei Pescatori), tel: 091 923 9867. Only accessible by boat; seasonal specialities on a lakeside terrace. Lake fish is fresh and especially good. Closed Oct–Apr; reservations recommended. €€€

La Tinera, Via dei Gorini 2, tel: 091 923 5219. Delicious Ticino cooking served in a rustic tavern on wooden benches. Closed Sun, last week in Jul and first three weeks in Aug. €

Malcesine

Trattoria Vecchia Malcesine, Via Pisort 6, tel: 045 740 0469. Local, seasonal dishes from a Michelin-starred restaurant. Outside service in summer with great views. Closed Wed, lunch (except Sun lunch and holidays Apr–Oct) and Feb; reservations essential. €€€–€€€€

Orta San Giulio

Leon d'Oro, Piazza Motta 41, tel: 0322 911991. The hotel's restaurant has a long, shady terrace on the water's edge overlooking the Isola. Good-value menu of local dishes; lake fish is a speciality. €€

Venus, Piazza Motta 50, tel: 0322 90362. Tables spill out onto the town's main piazza, overlooking the waterfront. There are very good pizzas as well as a *menu degustazione* for larger appetites. Closed Mon. €€

Villa Crespi, Via Fava 18, tel: 0322 911902. Antonio Cannavacciuolo's gourmet cuisine has earned him two Michelin stars. The food and service are faultless, the setting exquisite in this fairytale Moorish fantasy. Closed Mon; reservations essential. €€€€

Sacro Monte, Via Sacro Monte (1km/½ mile east of Orta San Giulio), tel: 032 290220. Set in the grounds of the Sacro Monte, this pleasing family-run restaurant has cosy, rustic rooms and an ivy-clad terrace with glorious views over the lake. Very good wine list. Closed Mon eve, Tues (except Aug), and Nov–Easter. €€–€€€

Al Sorriso, Via Roma 18, Soriso, (8km/5 miles south of Orta San Giulio), tel: 0322 983228. This hallowed restaurant in the tiny village of Soriso is the proud bearer of three Michelin stars – one of only five in the whole of Italy. Closed Tues, and two weeks in Jan and Aug; reservations essential. €€€€

Riva

Restel de Fer, Via Restel de Fer 10, tel: 0464 553481. Lake Garda fish specialities and folklore performances. Closed lunch, Tues and Nov–Jan. €€

Villa Negri, Via Bastione 31/35, tel: 0464 555061. Fish restaurant overlooking the lake; popular panoramic terrace in summer. Closed lunch and Tues Nov–Feb. €€€€

Al Volt, Via Fiume 73, tel: 0464 552570. Family-run with good service, romantic atmosphere and seasonal dishes. Specialises in meat as well as lake fish. Closed Mon, lunch in July, and mid-Feb–mid-Mar. €€

Salò

Lepanto, Lungolago Zanardelli 67, tel: 0365 20428. Excellent fish dishes, art nouveau surroundings and lovely terrace. Rooms also available. Closed Thurs and mid-Jan–Feb. €€–€€€

Trattoria alla Campagnola, Via Brunati 11, tel: 0365 22153. Family-run; home-made pasta and wild mushrooms in season. Closed Mon, lunch and 6 Jan–10 Feb; book for dinner. €€–€€€

Sirmione

Risorgimento, Piazza Carducci 5/6, tel: 030 916325. Lovely building with outdoor seating in summer. Closed Tues (except July–Aug), Feb, mid-Dec–7 Jan. €€–€€€

La Rucola, Vicolo Strentelle 7, tel: 030 916326. Superb cooking (one Michelin star), in an elegant atmosphere. Closed Thur and Fri lunch, and Jan–mid-Feb; must book. €€€–€€€€

Stresa

La Botte, Via Giuseppe Mazzini 6/8, tel: 0323 30462. A tiny restaurant, located in a narrow street just off the main piazza, offering a warm atmosphere and seasonal Piedmontese specialities such as local sausages and good pastas and pizzas. €–€€

L'Emiliano, Corso Italia 52, tel: 0323 31396. Intimate restaurant with local cheeses, and good pasta and lamb. €€

Piemontese, Via Mazzini 25, tel: 0323 30235. Excellent Piedmontese food and pretty garden. Closed Mon Dec–Jan, and Sun eve Oct–Mar. €€–€€€

Triangolo, Via Roma 61, tel: 0323 32736. Innovative cuisine in airy classical surroundings. *Al fresco* dining in summer. Closed Tues (except Aug) and Dec. €€–€€€

Torbole

Al Pescatore, Via Segantini 11, tel: 0464 505236. Open-air seafood bistro. Closed Mon lunch and Nov–Mar. €€

Piccolo Mondo, Via Matteoti 7, tel: 0464 505271. Good Trentino food is served in this highly acclaimed hotel-restaurant; there is a special menu with only apple dishes. Closed Tues (except summer) and three weeks in Feb. €€€

La Terrazza, Via Benaco 14, tel: 0464 506083. Excellent seafood served beside the lake; very popular summer terrace. Closed Tues (except June–Sept), Feb–Mar and Nov; must reserve in summer. €€–€€€

Terrazze, loc. Coe, tel: 0464 505301. Trentino specialities and good wine in a 19th-century Austrian 'fort'. €€–€€€

Toscolano-Maderno

La Tana, Via Aquilani 14, tel: 0365 644286. Great seafood served in pleasant trattoria. Closed Tues. €€

Varese

Ristorante Lago Maggiore, Via Corrobbio 19, tel: 0332 231182. Excellent cooking in an 18th-century palace. Closed Sun, Mon lunch, and July; booking essential. €€€

Verbania

Osteria dell' Angelo, Piazza Garibaldi 35, Pallanza, tel: 0323 556362. Good regional specialities, delicious risotto and lake fish. Closed Mon, and first week of Jan; booking advised. €€–€€€

Ristorante Milano, Corso Zanitello 2, tel: 0323 556816. Lovely location in a Liberty villa overlooking the lake and the Borromean islands. Good selection of local specialities and excellent wine list. €€–€€€

La Tavernetta, Via San Vittore 22, Intra (Verbania), tel: 0323 402635. Lovely old place with good, creative food. Outside dining in summer. Closed Tues and Nov. €€

Il Torchio, Via Manzoni 20, Pallanza, tel: 0323 503352. Good Italian food, Piedmontese specialities. Closed Wed, Thur lunch; booking advised. €€–€€€

Verona

Arche, Via Arche Scaligere 6, tel: 045 800 7415. First-class food, including seafood and black truffles. Closed Sun and Mon lunch, and 7–31 Jan; book ahead. €€€–€€€€

Il Desco, Via Dietro San Sebastiano 7, tel: 045 595358. Michelin-starred food in elegant surroundings. Closed Sun, Mon (except Mon eve in July, Aug and Dec), 25 Dec–10 Jan and two weeks in Jun; booking essential. €€€€

I Dodici Apostoli, Corticella San Marco 3, tel: 045 596999. Try the Venetian liver, wild mushrooms or king prawns. Closed Sun eve, Mon, 2–8 Jan and mid-June–early July. €€€–€€€€

Osteria La Fontanina, Portichetti Fontanelle, Santo Stefano 3, tel: 045 913305. Michelin-starred restaurant serving good-value and inventive food. Closed Sun and Mon lunch, one week in Jan, and Aug holidays; booking essential. €€€–€€€€

Re Teodorico, Piazzale Castel San Pietro, tel: 045 834 9990. Above the Teatro Romano. Closed Sun eve, Wed and 7–31 Jan. €€€–€€€€

ACTIVE HOLIDAYS

ANGLING

Official angling licences (valid for three months) must be bought from the Federazione Italiana della Pesca Sportiva. Angling permits are then issued locally. Local offices sell daily and weekly tickets. Fishing without a permit attracts a large fine.

CYCLING

Bicycles *(biciclette)* can be hired in Ticino at any major railway station. There is a signposted cycle route from Bellinzona to Ascona. For cyclists wishing to avoid hills, the best routes are those between the lakes, or the flat area south of Lake Garda.

Mountain bikes can also be hired in most places, but remember that a lot of mountain roads are closed between November and mid-April. For the less ambitious, the cable car from Malcesine on Lake Garda up to Monte Baldo also takes mountain bikes, saving an exhausting ascent and providing a superb trip back down.

The lakes are also a great area for cycle touring. Possible tours include complete circuits of either Maggiore or Como, which have the advantage of keeping mainly to level ground, or longer, and more challenging, tours linking several of the lakes by tackling the hills in between. For those who are really keen, the Lakes provide a very scenic access route to the high (over 2,000m/ 6,500ft) Alpine passes that lead into central Switzerland.

HANG-GLIDING

For courses in Lugano, contact Scuola Volo delta Lugano, tel: 092 822487. Near Lake Garda, the cable cars from Malcesine up to Monte Baldo and from Prada to Costabella take gliders up to 1,800m (5,900ft), allowing at least two flights a day. In the Garda region, contact Deltaland, loc. Platano di Caprino Veronese, tel: 045 623 0024. In Lugano you can contact: Club volo libero Ticino, c/o Roberto De Luigi, CH-6951 Pezzolo, www.para gliding-ticino.ch

HIKING AND CLIMBING

Compared with the serious hiking on offer in the high Alps, the Lakes region favours a gentle pace. Tucked into the Alpine foothills with balmy micro-climates, there are both high-level walks, often surrounded by Alpine mists, or more Mediterranean strolls closer to the shore.

The mountains around Lake Garda have well-marked paths and mountain huts *(rifugi)*, and include the Monte Baldo high-level route and Monte Pizzocolo on the western shore. From Malcesine, a cable car connects with a number of mountain paths and convenient *rifugi* for lunch. The enchanting villages of Tremosine and Tignale, perched on rocky crags, give walkers access to a series of inviting footpaths.

Lake Maggiore is well served by paths and cycle tracks, on both the Lombard and Piedmontese banks. From Laveno, a 5-km (3-mile) climb leads to Santa Caterina del Sasso. Around unspoilt Lake Iseo, Provaglio represents the start of a nature itinerary that takes in the peatbogs at the foot of Monte Provaglio and the reed beds that provide a refuge for many water birds.

The mountains of Ticino and around Lake Como are also easily accessible; a cable car connects the town of Como with Brunate, the starting point for scenic hiking in the hills. With its confluence of dramatic peaks and a serene lake shore, Bellagio is a good base. Two lovely walks are: from the lakeside Villa Melzi to Monte San Primo; and the 'Tremezzina' lakeside path (starting at Tremezzo) that links several villas and gardens.

The centre of mountaineering in the Garda region is Arco. The mountains around Maggiore provide climbers with routes of varying degrees of difficulty. Near Como, climbers should head for the Grigna; the town itself has a renowned climbing school that offers courses in mountaineering.

Maps and further information can be obtained from local tourist offices *(see page 119)*.

POTTERING AROUND

One of the nicest ways to enjoy the lakes' environment is simply to potter. The lakes are criss-crossed by many ferry routes, and taking a ride on these can be an end in itself. The many beautiful gardens open to visitors, often attached to grand villas, are also extremely pleasant places to while away the hours. This is all aided by the warm Mediterranean climate.

RIDING

Near Lake Garda, the best riding routes are to be found in the hilly country inland from Garda itself, along the slopes of Monte Baldo, or the river meadows along the Moncio. In the Maggiore region, there are riding schools in Losone (near Locarno), Quartino (near Magadino), Angera, Ghirla (Varesotto), Bodio (Lake Varese) and Magreglio and Canzo (both on Lake Como).

SKY-DIVING

For an exhilarating and altogether more adrenaline-fuelled aerial view of Lake Maggiore, try either the Club Parapendio Ticino in Locarno (tel: 091 752 1558) or the Scuola Volo Libero, Lugano (tel: 091 972 5821).

WINDSURFING

Lake Garda is a paradise for sailing and windsurfing due to the constant winds, the main ones being the Peler, which blows from the north in the early morning and the Ora, which blows from the south in the afternoon (noon–6pm approximately). The northern part of the Lake is good for sailing and windsurfing, while the south is well suited to rowing and canoeing, due to the calmer winds. The following firms hire sailing, windsurfing and canoeing equipment: Bardolino: Centro Nautico Bardolino Lungolago Preite 10, tel: 045 721 0816; Brenzone: Circolo Nautico Brenzone, Loc. Castelletto, tel: 045 743 0707; Castelletto: Hp Sports Noll Hans Peter, Via Imbarcadero, tel: 045 743 0707; Garda: Gruppa Vela LNI Garda, tel: 045 725 6377; Malcesine: Fraglia della Vela, Viale Roma 38, tel: 045 740 0274; Molini: Sunrise (windsurfing), tel: 045 740 1104; Campagnola: Wind Surf Bay, tel: 045 740 0311; Peschiera: Fraglia della Vela, Punta Marina, tel: 045 755 0727; Torri del Benaco: Yachting Club Torri, Via Marconi 1, tel: 045 722 5124.

Watersports
Windsurfing is available on Lakes Maggiore and Como, but nowhere is it more popular than the northern part of Lake Garda, around Torbole. Here the surfers get blown southwards by the Peler in the mornings and then up the lake again in the evenings by the Ora. In the summer months there are sometimes so many windsurfers around that ordinary swimming becomes almost impossible, but the water in the southern part of Lake Garda is much warmer for bathing anyway. All the lakes have facilities for every conceivable kind of other watersport including diving, water-skiing (not allowed on northern Lake Garda) and sailing; the larger resorts have schools and instructors.

PRACTICAL INFORMATION

Getting There

BY PLANE
Western Lakes (Maggiore, Orta, Como): Milan Malpensa, served by Alitalia (08705 448 259; www.alitalia.co.uk) from Heathrow and Manchester, easyJet (0905 821 0905; www.easyjet.com) from Gatwick, and British Airways (0870 850 9 850; www.ba.com) from Heathrow, London City, Birmingham, Bristol and Manchester. **Lake Como**: Milan Linate airport is served by BA and Alitalia from Heathrow and easyJet from Gatwick. **Lakes Como and Garda**: Bergamo's Orio al Serio airport (Milan's third airport) is served by Ryanair (0871 246 0000; www.ryanair.com) from Luton, Stansted, Liverpool, Newcastle and Prestwick, and also by Jet2 (0871 226 1737; www.jet2.com) from Leeds-Bradford. **Lake Garda**: airports within easy reach are Brescia, served by Ryanair from Stansted, and Verona, served by BA from Gatwick. **Lake Lugano**: Zurich airport, reached on Swiss (0845 601 0956; www.swiss.com/uk) from Heathrow, London City, Birmingham and Manchester, or on Darwin (00 800 1771 7777; www.darwinairline.com) from London City.

BY TRAIN
If travelling direct from the UK, the easiest place to head for is Milan. Take the Eurostar to the Gard du Nord in Paris, then change to the Gare du Lyon for overnight services to Milan through the Simplon Tunnel. Milan is connected by rail to Lake Maggiore, Varese, Como and Bergamo, as well as Brescia, the southern tip of Lake Garda and Verona, which are all on the main line to Venice. From Germany or Austria, a possibility for Lake Garda is via the Brenner Pass, to Rovereto or Verona, each of which has direct bus connections to the lake. For the Maggiore and Como region, there are hourly trains via Switzerland along the historic Gotthard Line. See www.raileurope.co.uk

BY CAR
Northern Italy is well connected to the rest of Europe by motorway. If you travel through Switzerland you need a *vignette* (motorway tax disc, valid for one year, approximate price £18; www.swisstravel system.co.uk). Drivers must always carry a driving licence, the car registration documents and insurance certificate. Breakdown services are usually free for members of automobile clubs. Seat-belts are compulsory. Fines for traffic offences such as illegal parking and speeding are high. The following speed limits generally apply in Italy: 50kmph (30mph) in built-up areas, 90kmph (55mph) on country roads, and 130kmph (75mph) on motorways *(autostrada)*. Speed limits are often lowered at weekends or on public holidays. Police checks are strict, and excessive speed as well as alcohol consumption (legal limit 0.08 percent) can cost motorists their licence – regardless of nationality.

Getting Around

BY CAR
Renting a car is probably cheaper than bringing your own, and there is no shortage of fly-drive packages, where cars can be collected on arrival. Alternatively, both international and local car hire firms are represented in the major centres. Driving along the narrow, winding mountain roads requires care and attention. Remember that the car nearest the mountain has priority. It is customary to use the horn to warn that you are about to overtake, and to warn of your presence on a blind bend. Many

of the roads in the area, particularly the one along the western shore of Lake Garda, disappear into tunnels. Throughout Italy, dipped headlights must be used at all times.

BY TRAIN
Near the lakes themselves, the following connections are possible: Locarno–Luino–Laveno–Sesto Calende; Simplon–Stresa–Sesto Calende; Laveno–Varese–Milan; Como–Milan; Como–Lecco; and Milan–Lecco– Colico. Keep an eye out for the various special offers available from the Swiss (www.sbb.ch/en) and the Italian railways (www.trenitalia.com/en). For connections from Milan to Lake Garda, remember that the fast express trains don't stop at Peschiera, Sirmione or Desenzano.

BY BUS
There are very good bus networks in Switzerland and Italy, and getting around the region poses few problems. The local tourist offices can provide timetables and general information.

BY BOAT
One of the best and most relaxing ways of seeing the lakes is from the deck of a steamer. All major towns on the Italian lakes have ferry connections for passengers, and a number of towns are linked by car ferry as well: Verbania–Laveno on Lake Maggiore; Menaggio–Bellagio–Varenna and Cadenabbia–Bellagio–Varenna on Lake Como; and Maderno–Torri del Benaco on Lake Garda. The Maggiore and Lugano steamers cross the border between Italy and Switzerland, so the usual border procedures apply. The larger vessels have on-board restaurants. A trip along the full length of Lake Garda, from Desenzano to Riva, takes around four and a half hours.

Cruises are a regular feature during the summer months, and disco ships are also common. Genuine old-fashioned paddle steamers are still used by some operators.

For general information on Navigation services across the lakes contact: Ministry of Transport and Navigation, Gestione Governativa Navigazione sui Laghi Maggiore, di Garda, di Como, Via Ludovico Ariosto 21, Milan, tel: (02) 467 6101, fax: (02) 4676 1059; www.navigazionelaghi.it

For information on Lake Orta, contact Navigazione Lago d'Orta, Via Simonotti 35, Borgomanero, tel: 0322 905698. For Lake Lugano contact Navigazione Lugano in Switzerland, tel: (0041) 91971 5223, fax: (0041) 91971 2793. For Lake Iseo, Navigazione Lago d'Iseo, Via Nazionale 16, Costa Volpino, tel: 0359 71483.

Facts for the Visitor

TRAVEL DOCUMENTS
Visitors from European Union countries require either a passport or identification card to enter Italy. Holders of passports from most other countries do not usually require visas for a period not exceeding three months.

CUSTOMS
There are no limits to the amount of goods that can be taken between EU member states. The following are

> **Souvenirs**
> Most souvenirs are of the gastronomic variety, with finest-quality olive oil, cheese, truffles, sausages, honey, wine and grappa usually topping the list. Bargains can also be had at flea markets in the larger towns; try to avoid the innumerable boutiques in the tourist resorts. Antiques markets can be a good place to buy special items cheaply. Ask at the local tourist information office about where and when they are held.

rough guidelines for items intended for personal use: 3,200 cigarettes, 200 cigars, 3kg of tobacco, 90 litres of wine, 110 litres of beer.

TOURIST INFORMATION

Here are the addresses of the Italian Tourist Office (www.enit.it):
UK: 1 Princes Street, London W1B 2AY, tel: 020 7408 1254.
US: 630 Fifth Avenue, Suite 1565, New York NY 10111, tel: 212 245 4822.

In Italy, contact the APT (Azienda di Promozione Turistica): APT **Verona**, Via Leoncino 61, 37121 Verona, tel: 045 806 8680, fax: 045 800 3638; APT **Garda/Trentino**, Giardini di Porta Orientale 8, 38066 Riva del Garda, tel: 0464 554444, fax: 0464 520308; APT **Como**, Piazza Cavour 17, 22100 Como, tel: 031 274064, fax: 031 261152; APT del **Varesotto**, Viale Ippodromo 9, 21100 Varese, tel: 0332 284624, fax: 0332 238093; APT del **Lago Maggiore**, Via Principe Tomaso 70/72, 28049 Stresa, tel: 0323 30150, fax: 0323 32561. APT **Bergamo**, Viale Vittorio Emanuele II 20, tel: 035 213185/242226; APT **Locarno**, Largo Zorzi 1, 6600 Locarno, tel: 091 791 00 91, fax: 091 785 1941.

Regional websites

Lombardy: www.inlombardia.it
Piedmont: www.regione.piemonte.it
Trentino: www.provincia.tn.it/apt
Lake Como: www.lakecomo.com
Lake Garda: www.lagodigarda.it
Lake Maggiore: www.lagomaggiore.it
Verona: www.tourism.verona.it

CONSULATES IN MILAN

UK: tel: 02 723001; www.embitaly.org.uk
US: tel: 02 290351; http://milan.usconsulate.gov/

CURRENCY AND EXCHANGE

The euro (€) is the official currency of Italy. Notes are denominated in 5, 10, 20, 50, 100 and 500 euros; coins in 1 and 2 euros and 1, 2, 5, 10, 20 and 50 cents.

Most credit cards, including Visa, MasterCard and American Express, are accepted in hotels, restaurants and shops and for air and train tickets and cash at any bank. All the larger towns in the region have ATMs ('Bancomat') that accept debit and credit cards.

> ### Public holidays
>
> 1 January, 6 January (Epiphany), Easter Sunday, Easter Monday, 25 April (National Day of Liberation), 1 May (Labour Day), Whit Sunday, 15 August (Assumption of the Virgin, *ferragosto*), 1 November (All Saints' Day), 8 December (Immaculate Conception), and 25 and 26 December (Christmas and St Stephen's Day).
>
> Many businesses close for some of August, and whole towns tend to close when a major festival is in progress.

TIPPING

This is expected, despite all-inclusive prices (approximately 10 percent).

OPENING TIMES

Generally, shops are open on weekdays and Sat 9am–7.30pm, with a lunch break 1–3.30pm. Many shops are closed on Monday mornings and another half-day per week.

Banks are open Mon–Fri 8.30am–1.30pm; some also open in the afternoon 2.45pm–3.45pm. Money can be exchanged at weekends in the railway stations and airports of the larger cities.

Museum opening hours vary considerably from place to place, and the times stated in this book are subject to change (check locally). State-owned museums are generally open daily 9am–2pm, and 9am–1pm on Sun and public holidays. They are often closed on Mon. Note: some state-owned and municipal museums allow free admission to visitors under 18 and over 60 years of age.

Churches are usually closed around lunchtime, roughly noon–3pm.

Petrol stations, apart from those on the motorways, are closed at lunchtime, on Sun and public holidays. Some have card-operated automatic pumps.

POSTAL SERVICES
Main post offices in major towns are open all day, some up to 7pm; otherwise Mon–Sat 8am–1.30pm. Stamps are sold at post offices as well as at bars and tobacconists; look for the white letter T on a blue background.

TELEPHONE
Calls can be made from phone centres run by the phone company TELECOM, or from public phones using coins or pre-paid phone cards *(scheda telefonica)*, which are available in various denominations from newsagents, tobacconists or TELECOM offices.

There is direct dialling to most countries, including: Australia 0061; United Kingdom 0044; US and Canada 001.

If making a phone call within Italy, note that the area or city codes are now dialled as part of the number, even when calling within the same city or area. Thus a Como number always has the code 031 attached, no matter where you're calling from. If you're calling Italy from abroad, you must dial the '0' of the area code after the country code (39).

Access numbers: AT&T: 172-1011, Sprint: 172-1877, MCCI: 172-1022.

TIME
One hour ahead of GMT, two hours ahead between March and October.

VOLTAGE
Usually 220v. Safety plugs cannot always be used. Specialist shops can provide adaptors *(spina di adatta-*

mento). American visitors will need a transformer.

CRIME
The lakes are relatively free of crime, but visitors should still take the usual precautions: don't leave any valuables inside your car, always lock the vehicle when you leave it, and leave your cash in the hotel safe. When out walking in big towns and cities keep a close eye on your cameras and handbags.

MEDICAL
The European Health Insurance Card (EHIC), available from post offices or at www.ehic.org.uk, entitles UK visitors to reciprocal medical treatment in Italy. There are similar arrangements for other members of EU countries. It may nevertheless be advisable to take out insurance for private treatment in case of accident. Holiday insurance and private patients schemes are recommended for non-EU visitors.

In case of minor ailments, chemists *(farmacie)* are well stocked with medicines, often sold without a prescription. *Farmacie*, which are normally open Mon–Fri 9am–1pm and 4–7pm, are identified by a sign displaying a green cross on a white background. At other times, the address of the nearest emergency chemist will be posted in the window.

EMERGENCIES
General Emergency Assistance (Ambulance, Fire, Police), tel: 113. Police Immediate Action, tel: 112. Breakdown service, tel: 116. Emergency medical assistance, ambulance, tel: 118.

WOMEN TRAVELLERS
Women often have to put up with unwanted male attention, but it is rarely dangerous. Ignoring comments and whistles is the best policy.

ACCOMMODATION

Whether you feel like sleeping in a 17th-century villa, a *casa rustica* or out on a campsite, Ticino, Lombardy and Piedmont all have a huge variety of accommodation to suit every taste.

On Lake Maggiore, the luxury hotels tend to be on the Swiss side and western shore, while smaller, family-run hotels are mostly on the eastern shore. On Lake Lugano and around Como, the luxurious hotels are usually magnificent old villas surrounded by extensive parks. Alongside these five-star establishments, there are numerous medium-priced ones with cable TV, swimming pools and air conditioning. Lake Garda has fewer five-star hotels than the other lakes.

Generally speaking, the nearer a lake a hotel is, the higher the price. Cheaper lodgings can be found in the towns and villages of the hinterland, away from the lakes, where there are plentiful hotels and also pensions and rooms let out by farmers (*agriturismo*); visit www.agriturismoinitalia.com. Campsites are usually right beside the lakes (the ones inland are a lot cheaper and quieter), and generally have all modern conveniences, although they can often be overcrowded in the summer months.

Anyone wishing to book self-catering accommodation can organise anything from a *casa rustica* to an enormous villa through a travel agent or by searching on the Internet.

HOTEL SELECTION

Hotels are officially classed into five categories: luxury; category I; category II; category III; and category IV. Lists of hotels and boarding-houses indicating their prices can be obtained from tourist offices. Rates – even within the same category – vary considerably depending on location.

We have categorised accommodation into three groups: €€€ = expensive; €€ = moderate; € = inexpensive.

Ascona (Switzerland)

Castello Seeschloss, Piazza G. Motta, tel: (41) 091 791 0161, www.castello-seeschloss.ch. Luxury hotel in an old castle, with a lakeside garden and pool. €€€

Tamaro, Piazza G. Motta 35, tel: (41) 091 791 0282, www.hotel-tamaro.ch. Patrician residence with an attractive courtyard, good restaurant and an 18th-century sun terrace. €€€

Bardolino

Cristina Color Hotel, Via Santa Cristina 5, tel: 045 621 0857, www.colorhotel.it. Colour-themed boutique hotel, very popular with a faithful following of clients. Swimming pool. Closed mid-Oct–late Mar. €€

Kriss Internazionale, Lungolago Cipriani 3, tel: 045 621 2433, www.hotelkriss.it. Situated in a prime position overlooking the lake, with its own private beach. Welcoming and attentive service. Closed Dec–Jan. €€–€€€

San Pietro, Via Madonnina 15, tel: 045 721 0588, www.san-pietro-hotel.com. Good-value hotel with a swimming pool, near the lake. Closed end Oct–mid-Mar. €€

Bellagio

Grand Hotel Villa Serbelloni, Via Roma 1, tel: 031 950216, www.villa serbelloni.it. Luxury hotel on Lake Como, with an excellent restaurant. The views, grounds and service are impeccable. Closed mid-Nov–Mar. €€€

La Pergola, Piazza del Porto 4, tel: 031 950263, www.lapergolabellagio.it. In the village of Pescalto, about a 10-minute walk from Bellagio. Simple, clean, family-run place overlooking the lake. Closed Nov–Mar. €€

Silvio, Via Carcano 10/12, 2km/1 mile south of Bellagio, tel: 031 950322, www.bellagiosilvio.com. A family-run small hotel with 21 rooms. Good restaurant with views across the lake and alfresco service in summer. Closed 20 Nov–20 Dec, 6 Jan–6 Mar. €€

Bergamo
Agnello d'Oro, Via Gombito 22, tel: 035 249883. Popular, small inn in the upper city with simple but comfortable rooms and a fine restaurant. €€
Excelsior San Marco, Piazza della Repubblica 6, tel: 035 366111, www. hotelsanmarco.com. Impressive modern hotel in the lower city with good service and facilities and roof garden. €€€

Como
Barchetta Excelsior, Piazza Cavour 1, tel: 031 3221, www.hotelbarchetta.it. Rather anonymous but redeemed by its central location. Some rooms overlook the lake. €€€
Grand Hotel Villa d'Este, Via Regina 40, Cernobbio, tel: 031 3481, www. villadeste.it. A 16th-century villa offering the ultimate in luxury, in beautiful parkland on the lakeside. Closed mid-Nov–Feb. €€€
Palace Hotel, Lungolario Trieste 16, tel: 031 23391, www.palacehotel.it. Lakeside hotel near the cathedral. €€€
Tre Re, Via Boldoni 20, tel: 031 265374, www.hoteltrere.com. Comfortable family-run *albergo* with pleasant rooms. Closed mid-Dec–early Jan. €€
Villa Flori, Via Cernobbio 12, tel: 031 33820, www.hotelvillaflori.com. Luxury hotel with mountain and lake views and a lovely terrace and gardens. Closed Nov–Feb. €€€

Desenzano del Garda
City, Via Nazario Sauro 29, tel: 030 991 1704, www.hotelcity.it. Family-run town hotel in a nice peaceful location (no restaurant). Closed 20 Dec–20 Jan. €–€€
Lido International, Via Tommaso dal Molin 63, tel: 030 914 1027, www.lidointernational.eu. Comfortable and reasonably priced with gardens, a terrace and swimming pool. Closed Nov–Jan. €€

Park Hotel, Lungolago Cesare Battisti 19, tel: 030 914 3351, www.parkhotelonline.it. Elegant hotel close to the lake. Tasteful rooms and good service. €€–€€€

Garda
Bisesti, Corso Italia 34, tel: 045 725 5766, www.hotelbisesti.com. Hotel close to the historical centre with simple, comfortable rooms. Pleasant, unpretentious atmosphere. Large garden with pool. Closed Nov–Feb. €–€€
Flora, Via Giorgione 27, tel: 045 725 5348, www.hotelflora.net. No restaurant but very friendly and great value. Closed mid-Sept–mid-May. €€
Regina Adelaide, Via San Francesco d'Assisi 23, tel: 045 725 5977, www.regina-adelaide.it. Beautiful rooms set in gardens with a swimming pool. Good restaurant. €€€

Gardone Riviera
Bellevue, Via Zanardelli 81, tel: 0365 290088, www.hotelbellevuegardone.com. A very comfortable hotel, overlooking the lake, with a swimming pool. Good value. Closed mid-Oct–Mar. €€
Dimora Bolsone, Via Panoramica 23, tel: 0365 21022, www.dimorabolsone.eu. Lovely country house dating to the 15th century, set in parkland. Just five rooms. Closed Dec–Feb. €€–€€€
Grand Hotel Gardone Riviera, Corso Zanardelli 84, tel: 0365 20261, www.grangardone.it. Luxury establishment

> ### The Borromean Islands
> For a romantic escape, you might consider staying on one of the Borromean islands in the middle of Lake Maggiore. If this appeals, and you feel like spoiling yourself, try the **Hotel Verbano**, Via Ugo Ara 12, Isola dei Pescatore, tel: 0323 30408, www.hotelverbano.it. The Isola dei Pescatore is one of the smallest and most romantic of the islands, and the Verbano has 12 old-fashioned but charming rooms, with breathtaking views over the lake. €€€

with a century of tradition and a Who's Who list of previous guests. Garden terraces overlooking the private sandy beach. Closed late Oct–Mar. €€€

Gargnano

Baia d'Oro, Via Gamberera 13, Villa (1km/½ mile south of Gargnano), tel: 0365 71171, www.hotelbaiadoro.it. Lovely old small hotel in a very peaceful location. Alfresco service on the terrace by the lake in summer. Closed Nov––Easter. €€

Grand Hotel a Villa Feltrinelli, Via Rimembranza 38–40, tel: 0365 798000, www.villafeltrinelli.com. Mussolini's last home before his demise is now a fabulous, opulent hotel with all modern facilities. Closed Nov–Mar. €€€

Villa Giulia, Viale Rimembranza 20, tel: 0365 71022, www.villagiulia.it. Quiet location next to lake. Closed mid-Oct––early Apr. €€€

Laveno

Il Porticciolo, Via Fortino 40, tel: 0332 667257, www.ilporticciolo.com. A well-known hotel-restaurant with modern rooms overlooking the lake – among the best in town. €€–€€€

Limone sul Garda

Ilma, Via Caldogno 1, tel: 0365 954041, www.hotelilma.it. Splendid lake and mountain views from light and airy rooms; pool. Closed Dec–Feb. €€

Park Hotel Imperial, Via Tamas 10/b, tel: 0365 954591, www.parkhotelimperial.com. Five-star luxury with all the facilities you would ever need. Closed three weeks in Dec, including Christmas. €€€

Locarno (Switzerland)

Albergo Elvetico, Via Vallemaggia 31, tel: (41) 091 756 6060. Pleasant three-star hotel within walking distance of the lake and old city centre. Large outside terrace. €€

Grand Hotel, Via Sempione 17, tel: (41) 091 743 0282. Grand hotel with every amenity including tennis courts and swimming pool. €€–€€€

Hotel Belvedere, Via Monti della Trinità 44, tel: (41) 091 751 0363, www.belvedere-locarno.com. This four-star hotel has a spa and is located in a lovely park with a pool. All rooms face the lake and have a balcony. €€€

Lugano (Switzerland)

Dischma, Vicolo Geretta 6, tel: (41) 091 994 2131, www.hotel-dischma.ch. Excellent value modern hotel with floral displays adorning the balconies. Very warm welcome. €–€€

Grand Hotel Villa Castagnola, Viale Castagnola 31, tel: (41) 091 973 2555, www.villacastagnola.com. Beautifully situated in tropical gardens by the lake; five-star luxury. Swimming pool, and health and beauty spa. €€€

Hotel Serpiano, 6867 Serpiano, tel: (41) 091 986 2000, www.serpiano.ch. Luxurious spa hotel with every facility set amid chestnut and oak forests with great views. Closed Dec–Feb. €€€

Villa Principe Leopoldo, Via Montalbano 5, tel: (41) 091 985 8855, www.leopoldohotel.com. Elegance and sumptuous decor in a 19th century mansion. Excellent restaurant. €€€

Walter au Lac, Piazza Rezzonico 7, tel: (41) 091 922 7425, www.walteraulac.ch. Established in 1888, a welcoming three-star hotel on the lakeside; all rooms face the lake. €€

Luino

Camin, Viale Dante 35, tel: 0332 530118, www.caminhotelluino.com. Elegant hotel surrounded by park at the centre of town. Large rooms, plushly furnished in Liberty style but with modern touches. Closed 21 Dec–end Jan €€€

Malcesine

Alpi, Localita Campogra018, tel: 045 740 0717. In a tranquil spot, yet not far from the centre, this comfortable hotel has a pleasant garden and swimming pool. Very good value. Closed mid-Nov–27 Dec and late Jan–Mar. €€

Maximilian, Val di Sogno, tel: 045 740 0317, www.hotelmaximilian.com. Quiet hotel in olive grove with tennis court and pool, just south of Malcesine. Closed Nov–Easter. €€€

Park Hotel Querceto, Via Panormaica 113 (5km/3 miles east of Malcesine), tel: 045 740 0344, www.park hotelquerceto.com. In a tranquil position, overlooking lake and mountains. An elegant hotel with 22 rooms, with a beautiful terrace for outdoor dining in summer. Closed mid-Oct–Apr. €€

Orta San Giulio

Hotel San Rocco, Via Gippini 11, tel: 0322 911977, www.hotelsanrocco.it. A perfect, peaceful lakeside hotel in a lovely 17th-century monastery. Highly acclaimed restaurant; swimming pool beside the lake. €€–€€€

Hotel Aracoeli, Piazza Motta 34; tel: 0322 905173. This central little hotel with nice lake views is minimalist and quirky, with seven individually designed rooms. Closed 20 Nov–15 Dec. €€

La Bussola, Via Panoramica 24, tel: 0322 911913, www.hotelbussolaorta.it. This welcoming family-run hotel has stupendous views. The rooms are charming and the superior rooms all have views of the lake. Closed Nov. €€

Villa Crespi, Via Fava 18, tel: 0322 911902, www.villacrespi.it. Best known for its Michelin-starred restaurant, there are also rooms offering Arabian Nights luxury in this Moorish 'palace'. Opulent furnishings, antique furniture and decadent bathrooms. €€€

Riva del Garda

Ancora, Via Montanara 2, tel: 0464 522131. Gracious, small *albergo* in the old centre. Well appointed and decorated rooms. €–€€

Hotel du Lac et du Parc, Viale Rovereto 44, tel: 0464 566600, www.hoteldulac-riva.it. A part-old, partmodern hotel on a part of Lake Garda where motorboats are banned. There are also holiday chalets in the spacious grounds. Closed Nov–Mar. €€€

Luise, Viale Rovereto 9, tel: 0464 550858. Good, comfortable, mediumsized hotel with pleasant restaurant (for hotel guests only) and swimming pool. Especially good for those who like mountain-biking. €€

Salò

Laurin, Viale Landi 9, tel: 0365 22022, www.laurinsalo.com. Stylish Liberty villa next to the lake. Gardens and pool. Closed Dec–mid Feb. €€€

Vigna, Lungolago Zanardelli 62, tel: 0365 520144, www.hotelvignasalo.com. A warm welcome in a historic, totally renovated hotel. The breakfast room has lovely, panoramic views. Closed mid-Dec–mid-Jan. €€

Sirmione

Corte Regina, Via Antiche Mura 11, tel: 030 916147, www.corteregina.it. Small, central *albergo*; good value and comfortable. There are visible Roman remains inside. Closed Dec–Mar. €

Fonte Boiola, Viale Marconi 11, tel: 030 916431, www.fonteboiola.com. Close to the heart of the old town; extremely good value. Has a lovely garden on the lake, a spa and a very pleasing restaurant. Closed 10–24 Dec. €€

Grand Hotel Terme, Viale Marconi 7, tel: 030 916261, www.termedisirmione. com. Five-star luxury, with its own thermal baths, set amid superb grounds. Closed early Jan–end Feb. €€€

Palace Hotel Villa Cortine, Via Grotte 12, tel: 030 990 5890, www.palace hotelvillacortine.it. A luxury neoclassical palazzo set in a lakeside park. Halfboard compulsory. Closed mid-Oct–mid-Mar. €€€

Sirmione, Piazza Castello 19, tel: 030 916331, www.termedisirmione.com. Very good service in the old centre, close to the lake. Pool. Closed Jan–Feb. €€€

Stresa

Grand Hotel des Iles Borromées, Lungolago Umberto I 67, tel: 0323 938938, www.borromees.it. Elegant luxury hotel in beautiful grounds above the

Borromean Islands. The hotel featured in Ernest Hemingway's *A Farewell to Arms*. €€€

Lido 'La Perla Nera', Viale Lido 15, tel: 0323 33611. Good value family-run establishment set in flower-filled gardens. Closed 17 Oct–23 Mar. €€

Torbole

Piccolo Mondo, Via Matteotti 7, tel: 0464 505271, www.hotelpiccolomondo torbole.it. Pleasant, comfortable and relaxing hotel. Closed two weeks in Feb and Nov. €€

Villa Verde, Via Foci del Sarca 15, tel: 0464 505274. A quiet, family-run three-star establishment, with swimming pool and garden. €€

Torri del Benaco

Al Caminetto, Via Gardesana 52, tel: 045 722 5524, www.alcaminetto.com. Small, family-run and close to the lake in the heart of town. Friendly and attentive service. Open Easter–Nov. €–€€

Gardesana, Piazza Calderini 20, tel: 045 722 5411, www.hotel-gardesana.com. Traditional hotel on the harbour, with excellent restaurant (open eve only Mar–Oct). Former guests include Maria Callas and André Gide. €€

Toscolano–Maderno

Maderno, Via Statale 12, tel: 0365 641070, www.hotelmaderno.it. Liberty-style hotel situated in a very pleasant, shady garden, near to the lake. Lovely outdoor veranda and swimming pool. Closed Nov–Mar. €€

Villa Cappellina, Via Statale 200, tel: 0365 643859, www.villacappellina.eu. Exclusive boutique hotel overlooking the lake. Closed Nov–Jan. €€–€€€

Varenna

Royal Victoria, Piazza San Giorgio 5, tel: 0341 815111. Lovely location on the lakeside, a traditional 19th-century hotel with enchanting gardens, terrace and pool. Good restaurant. €€–€€€

Varese

Bologna, Via Broggi 7, tel: 0332 234362, www.albergobologna.it. Family-run,

traditional and comfortable hotel, centrally located. Simple, very pleasant rustic atmosphere. 18 rooms. Closed first two weeks in Aug. €

Palace Grand Hotel Varese, Via Manara 11, Colle Campigli, tel: 0332 327100, www.palacevarese.it. Luxurious Art Nouveau hotel in central position, with its own grounds. €€–€€€

Verbania

Grand Hotel Majestic, Via Vittorio Veneto 32, Pallanza, tel: 0323 504305, www.grandhotelmajestic.it. Luxury hotel with attractive grounds, right next to the lake. Lovely island views. Closed Nov–Feb. €€€

Intra, Corso Mameli 133, Intra, tel: 0323 581393, www.verbaniahotel.it. Delightful small hotel close to the lake with comfortable, well-appointed rooms. No restaurant. €–€€

Verona

Aurora, Piazza dell Erbe 2, tel: 045 594717, www.hotelaurora.biz. Central little hotel with comfortable rooms. Breakfast is served on a lovely terrace overlooking the square. €

Due Torri Hotel Baglioni, Piazza Sant' Ananstasia 4, tel: 045 595044, www.baglionihotels.com. The most traditional five-star hotel in the city. Expensive luxury in a former palazzo. €€€

Gabbia d'Oro, Corso Porta Borsari 4/a, tel: 045 800 3060, www.hotelgabbiadoro.it. Elegant small hotel (8 rooms and 19 suites) offering five-star luxury. Probably the best hotel in Verona. No restaurant. €€€

Giulietta e Romeo, Vicolo Tre Marchetti 3, tel: 045 800 3554, www.giulietta eromeo.com. Very comfortable, but no restaurant. Some rooms have views of the Arena. €€

Victoria, Via Adua 6, tel: 045 590 0566, www.hotelvictoria.it. In the heart of the old quarter, a sensitively converted historic *palazzo* with Roman remains. Lovely bedrooms combining antiquity with modern decor. €€€

INDEX

OVER 250 DESTINATIONS IN 14 LANGUAGES

Let us be your guide

Your first visit – or a familiar destination? A short stay – or an extended exploration? Whatever your needs, there's an Insight Guide in a format to suit you. From Alaska to Zanzibar, we'll help you discover your world with great pictures, insightful text, easy-to-use maps, and invaluable advice.

www.insightguides.com